Self-Harm

h *Independence*

Educational Publishers
Cambridge

First published by Independence
PO Box 295
Cambridge CB1 3XP
England

British Library Cataloguing in Publication Data
Self-Harm – (Issues Series)
I. Firth, Lisa II. Series
362.2'8'0835'0941

ISBN 978 1 86168 388 5

Printed in Great Britain
MWL Print Group Ltd

Cover
The illustration on the front cover is by
Angelo Madrid.

CONTENTS

Introduction

Self-Harm is the one hundred and thirty-sixth volume in the **Issues** series. The aim of this series is to offer up-to-date information about important issues in our world.

Self-Harm looks at the problem of deliberate self-injury, as well as the issue of suicide.

The information comes from a wide variety of sources and includes:
Government reports and statistics
Newspaper reports and features
Magazine articles and surveys
Website material
Literature from lobby groups
and charitable organisations.

It is hoped that, as you read about the many aspects of the issues explored in this book, you will critically evaluate the information presented. It is important that you decide whether you are being presented with facts or opinions. Does the writer give a biased or an unbiased report? If an opinion is being expressed, do you agree with the writer?

Self-Harm offers a useful starting-point for those who need convenient access to information about the many issues involved. However, it is only a starting-point. Following each article is a URL to the relevant organisation's website, which you may wish to visit for further information.

* * * * *

Understanding self-harm

Information from Mind

'I belong to a women's self-harm support group. The group was the start of changing my life. The encouragement and support from both has given me the strength and courage to continue my life, and I now value myself. I still self-harm, but nowhere near as much as I used to. By talking about it, I am learning to deal with my feelings.'

'I am a survivor of both sexual abuse and self-injury. I no longer self-injure, but it has been a long struggle to try to acknowledge and work through emotions that once felt overwhelming in their power.'

'Self-harm involves all of us on some level. We may all punish, distract or numb ourselves, as a way of dealing with difficult feelings or situations.'

This article is for anyone who self-harms, their friends and family. It should give readers a greater understanding and knowledge of the condition and of what they can do to help overcome it.

What is self-harm?

Self-harm is a way of expressing very deep distress. Often, people don't know why they self-harm. It's a means of communicating what can't be put into words or even into thoughts and has been described as an inner scream. Afterwards, people feel better able to cope with life again, for a while.

Self-harm is a broad term. People may injure or poison themselves by scratching, cutting or burning their skin, by hitting themselves against objects, taking a drug overdose, or swallowing or putting other things inside themselves. It may also take less obvious forms, including taking stupid risks, staying in an abusive relationship, developing an eating problem, such as anorexia or bulimia, being addicted to alcohol or drugs, or simply not looking after their own emotional or physical needs.

These responses may help you to cope with feelings that threaten to overwhelm you; painful emotions, such as rage, sadness, emptiness, grief, self-hatred, fear, loneliness and guilt. These can be released through the body, where they can be seen and dealt with. Self-harm may serve a number of purposes at the same time. It may be a way of getting the pain out, of being distracted from it, of communicating feelings to somebody else, and of finding comfort. It can also be a means of self-punishment or an attempt to gain some control over life. Because they feel ashamed, afraid, or worried about other people's reactions, people who self-harm often conceal what they are doing rather than draw attention to it.

It's worth remembering that most people behave self-destructively at times, even if they don't realise it. Perfectly ordinary behaviour, such as smoking, eating and drinking too much, or working long hours, day after day, can all be helping people to numb or distract themselves and avoid being alone with their thoughts and feelings.

Why do people harm themselves?

A person who self-harms is likely to have gone through very difficult, painful experiences as a child or young adult. At the time, they probably had no one they could confide in, so didn't receive the support and the emotional outlet they needed to deal with it. The experience might have involved physical violence, emotional abuse, or sexual abuse. They might have been neglected, separated from someone they loved, been bullied, harassed, assaulted, isolated, put under intolerable pressure, made homeless, sent into care, into hospital or to other institutions.

Experiences like these erode self-esteem. Emotions that have no outlet may be buried and blocked completely out of awareness. If a trusted adult betrays or abuses them, and there are no other witnesses, children will often blame themselves. They turn their anger inwards. By the time they become adults, self-injury can be a way of expressing their pain, punishing themselves, and keeping memories at bay.

There is often an absence of pain during the act of self-injury, rather like the absence of sensation that often occurs during abuse or trauma. The body produces natural opiates, which numb it and mask the emotions, so that little is felt or realised consciously.

A badly traumatised person may end up feeling quite detached from their feelings and their body. Some may injure themselves to maintain that sense of being separate, and to convince themselves that they aren't vulnerable. Others may injure themselves in order to feel something and know that they are real and alive.

Self-harm is about trying to stay alive, despite the pain people are in

Healthcare professionals have been criticised for assuming that people who self-harm require no anaesthetic for stitching wounds. This is just one of the myths exploded in new guidelines on self-harm, developed by NICE (the National Institute for Clinical Excellence). Similarly, professionals sometimes make assumptions about why someone has injured themselves, particularly if they have done it before. But the meaning is different for each person, each time they self-harm. It is not a sign, in itself, that someone has a mental health problem.

Who is most likely to self-harm?

According to recent research, the majority are young women, although the percentage of young men seems to be on the increase. Self-harming behaviour is also significant among minority groups discriminated against by society. Someone who has mental health problems is more likely to self-harm. So are those who are dependent on

drugs or alcohol, or who are faced with a number of major life problems, such as being homeless, a single parent, in financial difficulty or otherwise living in stressful circumstances. One important common factor is a feeling of helplessness or powerlessness.

Recent research focusing on young people suggests that 10 per cent of 15- to 16-year-olds have self-harmed, usually by cutting themselves, and that girls are far more likely to self-harm than boys. The most common reason is 'to find relief from a terrible situation'. Young people are often under great pressure within their families, from school and among their peers. Many young people report having friends who also self-harm.

The research suggests that young people who self-harm are much more likely to have low self-esteem, to be depressed and anxious. They seem to be facing more problems in life, but may be less good at coping with them. They may retreat into themselves, feeling angry, blaming themselves, tending to drink and smoke too much and to use more recreational drugs. They confide in fewer friends, and tend not to talk to their parents or other adults, or to ask for the help they need.

Physical, emotional or sexual abuse

Women often find themselves in a caring role, putting their own needs last. This can grossly undermine their sense of worth, their opinions and strengths. In due course, a woman may come to feel she is an unimportant, silent witness to the abuses she has to endure. She may lose her sense of identity, power and rights. To survive, she may cut herself off from her real needs. If the focus for this is the size and shape of her body, she may drastically restrict what she eats.

If men conform to the macho stereotype that expressing emotion is a weakness, it can leave them unable to feel their feelings, and detached from that side of themselves. They may have less difficulty showing anger than women, but if they are in prison, where pent-up feelings can't be released, men are more likely to turn to self-harm, especially if they have been abused.

Is self-harm an attempt to commit suicide?

Self-harm is about trying to stay alive, despite the pain people are in. Although there is a relationship between self-harm and suicide, many more people self-harm than kill themselves, and most people don't hurt themselves so badly as to risk their lives. Of those who do, suicide may not have been their intention; it's the feelings they want to wipe out.

Whether someone wants to live or die may seem to be a straightforward choice. But some people are suspended in a grey state of survival, where choices and decisions are kept on hold. This is where self-harm happens.

For those who self-harm, surviving is subject to rigid controls; feelings are suppressed for fear of what may lie behind them. If living means having to cope with acutely painful feelings and memories, and there is not enough support available, the choice not to be alive may be more understandable. When someone you care about talks about death, it's natural to fear they may go through with it, but these are the very feelings they need to explore. Remember that human beings have an enormous capacity to survive great pain.

Is self-harming behaviour attention-seeking?

Because it can be hard to understand, healthcare professionals, friends and relatives sometimes mistakenly regard people who self-harm with mistrust or fear and see their behaviour as attention-seeking and manipulative. If someone you know self-harms, you may feel helpless when faced with their wounds, and your own feelings and fears about the situation may cause you to blame them instead of supporting them. Bear in mind they may be using the only way they can to communicate their plight and to get the attention, care and comfort they need. However upsetting it may be for you, it doesn't necessarily mean this is their intention. Whether people have deep wounds or slight injuries, the problem they represent should always be taken very seriously. The size of the wound isn't a measure of the size of the conflict inside.

Because it can be hard to understand, people sometimes mistakenly regard people who self-harm with mistrust or fear and see their behaviour as attention-seeking and manipulative

---

What triggers it?

You may harm yourself once or twice at a particularly difficult time in your life, and never do so again. But self-harming can become an ongoing way of coping with current problems and may occur regularly, on a monthly, weekly, or daily basis, depending on circumstances. The trigger could be a reminder of the past, such as an anniversary, which sets off a hidden memory, or something unexpected could happen to cause a shake-up. But sometimes, ordinary life is just so difficult that self-harm is the only way to cope with it.

What can I do to stop self-harming?

The single most important thing to remember is that you have choices: stopping self-injury can begin now.

⇨ Knowledge is power. Gather as much information as possible about your own behaviour. Keep notes of what is going on when you feel the need to harm yourself, so that you can identify, over a period of time, specific thoughts which come up. It's also useful to keep a daily diary of events and feelings, and to record how you

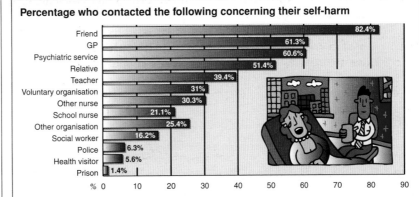

Contact and help-seeking

Percentage who contacted the following concerning their self-harm

	%
Friend	82.4%
GP	61.3%
Psychiatric service	60.6%
Relative	51.4%
Teacher	39.4%
Voluntary organisation	31%
Other nurse	30.3%
School nurse	21.1%
Other organisation	25.4%
Social worker	16.2%
Police	6.3%
Health visitor	5.6%
Prison	1.4%

% 0 10 20 30 40 50 60 70 80 90

Notes: people who visited the National Inquiry into Self-Harm's website were asked to fill in a detailed multiple choice questionnaire. A total of 142 young people aged from 13 upwards, with an average age of 20, completed questionnaires. There were 137 females and 5 males. Source: The National Inquiry into Self-harm, 'Truth Hurts' report, 2006.

cope with or channel powerful emotions of anger, pain or happiness.

⇨ Try to talk about your feelings with someone supportive. Even though you may feel you are alone, there are others who can understand your pain and help to boost your strength and courage. Many people find that joining a support group of people with similar problems is an important step towards making themselves feel better, and changing their lives. If there are no appropriate support groups in your area, your local Mind associations may be able to help start one.

⇨ Work on building up your self-esteem. Remember you are not to blame for how you feel; your self-injury is an expression of powerful negative feelings. It's not your fault. Make lists of your feelings, and then write positive statements about yourself, or the world around you. If you can't think of any, ask friends to write things they like about you. Keep these in a place so that they are visible. Make a tape of your own voice saying something affirming or reading your favourite stories or poems. Hearing your own voice can be soothing, or you can ask someone you trust to record their voice reading to you.

⇨ Try to find ways to make your life less stressful, give yourself occasional treats, eat healthily, get plenty of sleep and build physical activity into your life, because this is known to boost self-esteem and lift low moods.

⇨ Have the telephone numbers of friends, or local and national helplines where you can find them easily, if you need to talk to somebody in a crisis.

⇨ Think about your anger and what you do with it. If you weren't busy being angry with yourself, who would you really be angry with? Write a list of people who have caused you to feel like this. Remind yourself you deserve good things in life, not punishment for what others have done to you.

⇨ Line up a set of cushions to represent people who caused you pain. Tell them how they hurt you and that you don't deserve punishment. Kicking or hitting cushions is good. Try to do this with someone else, if possible, so that the experience is shared and you do not hurt yourself.

⇨ Creativity is a powerful tool against despair. This doesn't have to be about making something. Whatever lifts you out of your pain and makes you feel good is creative. If you feel like it, try drawing or painting how you feel. Some people draw on themselves, using bright body colours.

⇨ If you feel the need to self-harm, focus on staying within safe limits. A supportive GP will give you good advice on minimising and caring for your injuries and help you to find further help.

⇨ Reprinted from 'Understanding Self Harm' by permission of Mind (National Association for Mental Health) www.mind.org.uk
© Mind 2005

Self-harm and young people

Information from the Mental Health Foundation

Self-harm among young people is a major public health issue in the UK. It affects at least one in 15 young people, blights the lives of young people and seriously affects their relationships with families and friends. It presents a major challenge to all those in services and organisations that work with young people, from schools through to hospital accident and emergency departments.

What is self-harm?

Self-harm describes a wide range of things that people do to themselves in a deliberate and usually hidden way. In the vast majority of cases self-harm remains a secretive behaviour that can go on for a long time without being discovered. Self-harm can involve:

⇨ cutting
⇨ burning
⇨ scalding
⇨ banging or scratching one's own body
⇨ breaking bones
⇨ hair pulling
⇨ ingesting toxic substances or objects.

Why is self-harm an issue for young people?

Although some very young children are known to self-harm and some adults too, the available research evidence indicates that average age of onset is 12 years old. The evidence also shows that the rates of self-harm in adults aged 25 years and over are relatively low, so that the majority of young people who self-harm are aged between 11 and 25 years.

Why do young people self-harm?

It is important to recognise that self-harm is a symptom of underlying mental or emotional distress. Young people who self-harm mainly do so because they have no other way of coping with problems in their lives. The evidence about the reasons why young people self-harm shows that there are a wide range of factors that might contribute. Very often it appears – based on evidence from young people themselves – there may be multiple triggers, often daily stresses, rather than one significant change or event. Factors can include:

⇨ feeling isolated
⇨ academic pressures
⇨ suicide or self-harm by someone close to the young person
⇨ family problems, including parental separation or divorce
⇨ being bullied
⇨ low self-esteem.

> **Hospital records show that some 142,000 young people present at accident and emergency departments each year as a result of their self-harm but this is only part of the picture**

But self-harm is not a good way of dealing with such problems. It provides only temporary relief and does not deal with the underlying issues.

How common is self-harm among young people?

There is relatively little research evidence about the prevalence of self-harm among young people. Hospital records show that some 142,000 young people present at accident and emergency departments each year as a result of their self-harm but

this is only part of the picture. The majority of young people who self-harm will either not harm themselves in a way that needs medical treatment or they will deal with it themselves.

The research evidence that is available shows that between one in 12 and one in 15 young people self-harm in the UK. Some research suggests that the UK has the highest rate of self-harm in Europe.

Can self-harm among young people be prevented?

There is increasing evidence showing that there are ways to prevent self-harm among young people. Anti-bullying strategies and whole-school approaches designed to improve the general mental health and wellbeing of young people appear to have a positive effect, though there is no specific evidence as yet on their impact on self-harm.

Evidence from young people themselves suggests that social isolation – and believing that they are the only one that has self-harmed – can be a key factor in self-harm for some. It is likely that better information for young people about self-harm would increase their understanding and might help reduce or prevent self-harm. Similarly, better awareness and understanding among parents, teachers and others who come into contact with young

people is also likely to have a positive impact.

Do we have good responses to young people who self-harm?

There are a wide range of services across the UK for young people who self-harm. Anecdotal evidence suggests that many young people benefit very much from these, but to date there is not a strong evidence base to demonstrate their effectiveness.

There is stronger evidence – mostly direct from young people – that finding ways to distract from, or alternatives to, self-harm can

be very important for many young people. Distraction techniques that are reported as being effective for some young people include using a red pen to mark rather than cutting, rubbing with ice, hitting a punch bag or flicking elastic bands on the wrist.

Conclusion

Self-harm among young people is a serious public health challenge. There is a need for much better data about prevalence. There is also a need for better awareness and understanding of self-harm and

its underlying causes both among young people themselves and those who come into contact with them. Stronger and clearer evidence about what might prevent self-harm and about effective responses to self-harm among young people is also needed. *Written in 2006*

⇨ Reproduced from the Mental Health Foundation website with their permission. There is more information about self-harm at http://www.mentalhealth.org.uk/ campaigns/self-harm-inquiry/

© *Mental Health Foundation*

Teenagers' epidemic of self-harm

A new study suggests that one in 12 British children deliberately hurt themselves – the highest rate in Europe. Amelia Hill reports

A hidden epidemic of self-harm is affecting teenagers across Britain, with one adolescent in 12 deliberately injuring themselves on a regular basis.

The most comprehensive report into the issue, to be published tomorrow, will say that there are likely to be around two children in every classroom who self-harm. 'We have the highest rate of self-harm in Europe, but the universal misunderstanding about self-harm is so overwhelming that numbers will rise even further unless we act immediately,' said Catherine McLoughlin, chairwoman of the first ever national inquiry into self-harm among young people. She said that some reports suggested up to one in five adolescents were 'engaging in this self-destructive behaviour', a subject that was surrounded in 'guilt and secrecy'.

The panel discovered that children as young as five were deliberately hurting themselves, but said family and friends were often unaware that someone close to them was injuring themselves.

The inquiry, set up two years ago by the Camelot Foundation, the lottery firm's charitable arm, and the

Mental Health Foundation, spoke to more than 350 organisations and individuals. It brought together all available work on self-harm and also commissioned research. The report, *Truth Hurts*, will say that victims who seek help are often met with ridicule or hostility. 'This is a hidden epidemic of horrific proportions and we know virtually nothing about why it happens or how to stop it,' said McLoughlin. 'Basically, we understand about as much about self-harm as we did about anorexia 20 years ago.'

It emerged yesterday that people who self-harm are being allowed to cut themselves under the supervision of nurses in a pilot scheme being carried out by the South Staffordshire NHS Trust. It is hoped that supervision, rather than prohibition, will help patients find better ways of dealing with their problems.

Consultant nurse Chris Holley, who is organising the pilot, said guidelines had been drawn up to ensure that it took place in a safe way and was accompanied by efforts to encourage people who self-harm to stop.

Young people consulted for the *Truth Hurts* inquiry reported a

range of factors that had triggered self-harming, including bullying, not getting on with parents, stress and worrying about academic performance and exams. Other reasons cited included family breakdown, bereavement, problems to do with race, culture or religion, and low self-esteem.

A hidden epidemic of self-harm is affecting teenagers across Britain, with one adolescent in 12 deliberately injuring themselves on a regular basis

---

The range of reasons makes prevention difficult but when young people themselves try to get help, McLoughlin said, they are often met with reactions ranging from panic and revulsion to disgust and condemnation.

'Over and over again, the young people told us that their experience of asking for help often made their situation worse,' said McLoughlin. 'Others were met with ridicule or hostility from the professionals they turned to for help.'

Linda Dunion, director of the See Me campaign, which seeks to raise awareness of the issue in Scotland, agrees that the stigma of self-harm discourages young people from seeking help. 'Our research shows that over 40 per cent of adults think young people who self-harm are attention-seeking, one in three feel they are manipulative and 15 per cent believe it is the sign of a failed suicide attempt.'

But self-harm is a sign of a young person struggling to survive, says Jackie Cox, a psychologist and counsellor at Harrow school and consultant for Etch Teacher Training, a specialist organisation helping teachers to deal with difficult issues. 'Self-harm is a sign of emotional distress,' she said. 'It is a survival mechanism that young people use to cope with underlying emotional and psychological trauma.'

One teenager who wished to remain anonymous said his self-harm was a method of survival. 'It was a way to get rid of the hurt, anger and pain,' he said. 'But the rush it gave, the sense of feeling better, was always so short-lived that I had to do it many times. I've been through days when I haven't been able to get up in the morning and function without self-harm,' he added. 'I don't know how to release my feelings in any other way. Without self-harm, I doubt I would be alive now.'

Stigmatising young people who self-harm when they are most in need of help could drive their behaviour even further underground, where it could increase in severity, says Cox.

'Self-harm can trigger chemicals that bring about a very positive feeling of calm and wellbeing,' she said. 'But greater levels of harm often have to be inflicted to achieve the same effect, which can lead to an injury requiring professional treatment, or worse.'

McLoughlin hopes the report will be used as an agenda for change across the government, as well as education, health and social service groups.

'Self-harm is a sign of emotional distress. It is a survival mechanism that young people use to cope with underlying emotional and psychological trauma'

Among its demands are calls for a 'Healthy Schools Standard' that specifically addresses issues of self-harm, and a nationwide programme of training for all adults working with children.

In addition, the panel will press for the launch of a national campaign aimed at removing the stigmas surrounding self-harm.

The Mental Health Foundation is to set up a training centre for all those working with young people, while the Camelot Foundation will commission a web-based centre of excellence on self-harm, making up-to-date information easily accessible on a nationwide basis.

'It is time to stop passing judgment and start acting,' said McLoughlin. 'Secrecy and shame need to be replaced with understanding and support. We can no longer ignore the fact that self-harm is blighting the lives of our young people.'

Case study: 'I feel guilty about it, but it was the only way I could keep going' Lisa, age 13
'I still don't fully understand why I began cutting my wrists. I was 12 years old when I began, and pretty depressed, angry and isolated. One day, I accidentally hit my hand really hard against my bed and experienced this sudden feeling of relief. Then for some reason I decided to cut myself to see if I could make the good feelings last longer.

'The first time I cut myself, I barely made a mark but I did feel better, so I did it again a couple of days later but that time, I cut a bit deeper. I began cutting myself once a week on average. I felt guilty about what I was doing but it became the only way I could keep going. I really wanted help; I wanted to stop but didn't know who I could ask.

'I hid what I was doing for months, but one night my mum came to tuck me up and saw my scars. I wasn't relieved she had found out: I didn't cut myself as a cry for help and the idea of having to stop was terrifying. Now, I am glad she found out because otherwise, I would have continued. Eventually, I might have accidentally cut too deeply and ended up in hospital.

'Now I'm getting counselling, I haven't cut myself for nine months. But when I was upset recently, I deliberately punched the wall so hard my knuckles bled. Stopping self-harming is far harder than it ever was to start. I want to stop but I struggle every day.'
26 March 2006
© Guardian Newspapers Limited 2007

WHY DIDN'T YOU TELL US ABOUT IT?

I WAS AFRAID YOU WOULDN'T UNDERSTAND... THAT YOU'D LAUGH AT ME...

Girls and self-harm

One in ten teenage girls have self-harmed, study shows

One in ten teenage girls self-harm each year and the problem is far more widespread than was previously thought, shows the largest-ever study of self-harm amongst 15- and 16-year-olds in England.

In a survey of more than 6,000 15- and 16-year-old school pupils, researchers found that girls are four times more likely to have engaged in deliberate self-harm compared to boys, with 11 per cent of girls and three per cent of boys reporting that they had self-harmed within the last year.

Previous estimates for the amount of self-harm in the country were based on the 25,000 presentations at hospitals in England and Wales each year that are the result of deliberate self-poisoning or self-injury amongst teenagers.

However, research by academics from the universities of Bath and Oxford has found that only 13 per cent of self-harming incidents reported by the pupils had resulted in a hospital visit.

Although self-poisoning is the most common form of self-harm reported in hospitals, the study revealed that self-cutting was the more prevalent form of self-harm (64.5 per cent), followed by self-poisoning through overdose (31 per cent).

'The study shows that deliberate self-harm is common amongst teenagers in England, especially in girls who are four times more likely to self-harm than boys,' said Dr Karen Rodham from the Department of Psychology at the University of Bath.

'Until now, most studies of deliberate self-harm in adolescents in the UK have been based on the cases that reach hospital.

'We have found that the true extent of self-harm in England is significantly wider than that.'

Professor Keith Hawton from the Centre for Suicide Research at the University of Oxford, who directed the project, said: 'This study provides more information about why young people engage in deliberate self-harm and helps us to recognise those at risk, to develop explanatory models and to design effective prevention programmes.

'In many cases, self-harming behaviour represents a transient period of distress, but for others it is an important indicator of mental health problems and a risk of suicide.

'It is important that we develop effective school-based initiatives that help tackle what has become a most pressing health issue for teenagers.'

One in ten teenage girls self-harm each year and the problem is far more widespread than was previously thought

---

The research, which was carried out with Samaritans, has been published in the new book, *By their own young hand*, which includes practical advice for teachers on how to detect young people at risk – based on the evidence collected by the academics.

The book also suggests advice on coping with the aftermath of self-harm or attempted suicide in schools, and advice on designing training courses for teachers.

The research took place in 41 schools in Oxfordshire, Northamptonshire and Birmingham in 2000 and 2001.

Pupils were asked to complete a 30-minute questionnaire which explored issues surrounding self-harm and suicidal thinking – together with other personal factors such as depression, anxiety, impulsivity and self-esteem.

Those who reported self-harm were asked to provide a description of the act, its motivation and its consequences.

'The reasons why boys and girls decide to self-harm are varied but the most frequent motive expressed by both males and females was as a means of coping with distress,' said Dr Rodham.

For both sexes there was an incremental increase in deliberate self-harm with increased consumption of cigarettes or alcohol, and all categories of drug use.

Self-harm was more common in pupils who had been bullied and was strongly associated with physical and sexual abuse in both sexes.

Also, pupils of either sex who had recently been worried about their sexual orientation had relatively higher rates of self-harm.

The majority of those who said they self-harmed said that it was an impulsive act rather than something they had thought about for a long time.

Almost half of those who cut themselves, and over a third who took overdoses, said that they had thought about harming themselves for less than an hour beforehand.

Of those with a history of deliberate self-harm, 20 per cent reported that no one knew about it

This means that there is often little time for intervention once thoughts of self-harm have been fully formulated.

Of those with a history of deliberate self-harm, 20 per cent reported that no one knew about it and 40 per cent of those who reported thinking about self-harm had not talked to anyone about it or tried to get help.

The vast majority of pupils said that their friends were the people they felt that they could talk to about things that bothered them and those who had self-harmed most often turned to their friends.

'This responsibility places a great burden on adolescents to support their peers, yet most adolescents have not in any way been coached in how best to do this,' said Professor Hawton.

'Attention to this aspect of support for adolescents should be an essential part of mental health education in schools, and it is great to see the development of the wellness programmes currently being trialled in some schools.

'Whilst efforts to encourage adolescents to seek help through friends, family, help lines and clinical services are very relevant, prevention should be focused on reducing the problems that lead to thoughts of self-harm.

'This is where school-based initiatives can make the most important contribution to this important aspect of mental health.'

The research was funded by a £242,000 grant from the Community Fund.

Notes

By their own young hand – deliberate self-harm and suicidal ideas in adolescents is written by Keith Hawton & Karen Rodham, with Emma Evans, and is published by Jessica Kingsley Publishers (ISBN 1 84310 230 7, 264pp, pb £17.99).

The University of Bath is one of the UK's leading universities, with an international reputation for quality research and teaching. In 16 subject areas the University of Bath is rated in the top ten in the country. View a full list of the university's press releases: http://www.bath.ac.uk/news/releases *23 August 2006*

⇨ The above information is reprinted with kind permission from the University of Bath. Visit www.bath.ac.uk for more information.
© *University of Bath*

Myths and stereotypes

Information from the National Inquiry into Self-harm among Young People – an extract from 'The truth about self-harm'

There are lots of myths attached to self-harm. This isn't surprising – myths and misunderstandings often arise when a problem is, like self-harm, poorly understood.

The vast majority of young people who self-harm are not trying to kill themselves – they are trying to cope with difficult feelings and circumstances

Negative stereotypes can be powerful. They need to be challenged because they stop young people from coming forward for help. They also mean that professionals, family and friends are much more likely to react

in a hostile way to young people who self-harm.

Some of the most common stereotypes are that self-harm is about 'attention seeking'. Most self-harm is actually done in secret, for a long time, and it can be very hard for young people to find enough courage to ask for help.

Self-harm is sometimes seen as a group activity – especially when young people are 'goths'. But it's very rarely a group activity. Young people told the Inquiry that they couldn't say how many people they knew self-harmed, because no one wants to talk about it. The Inquiry could find no evidence to support the belief

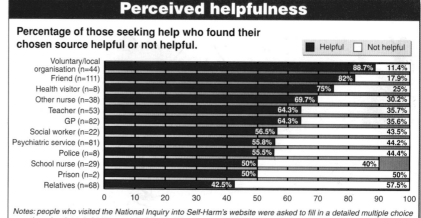

Perceived helpfulness

Percentage of those seeking help who found their chosen source helpful or not helpful.

■ Helpful ☐ Not helpful

Source	Helpful	Not helpful
Voluntary/local organisation (n=44)	88.7%	11.4%
Friend (n=111)	82%	17.9%
Health visitor (n=8)	75%	25%
Other nurse (n=38)	69.7%	30.2%
Teacher (n=53)	64.3%	35.7%
GP (n=82)	64.3%	35.6%
Social worker (n=22)	56.5%	43.5%
Psychiatric service (n=81)	55.8%	44.2%
Police (n=8)	55.5%	44.4%
School nurse (n=29)	50%	40%
Prison (n=2)	50%	50%
Relatives (n=68)	42.5%	57.5%

Notes: people who visited the National Inquiry into Self-Harm's website were asked to fill in a detailed multiple choice questionnaire. A total of 142 young people aged from 13 upwards, with an average age of 20, completed questionnaires. There were 137 females and five males. Source: The National Inquiry into Self-harm, 'Truth Hurts' report, 2006.

that this behaviour may be part of a particular youth sub-culture.

Is self-harm linked to suicide?

It is often the belief that self-harm is closely linked to suicide that frightens people most. But the vast majority of young people who self-harm are not trying to kill themselves – they are trying to cope with difficult feelings and circumstances – for many it is a way of staying alive. Many people who commit suicide have self-harmed in the past, and this is one of the many reasons that self-harm must be taken very seriously.

How do people self-harm?

There are lots of ways of self-harming. The most common is cutting yourself. People who self-harm tend to go to great lengths to keep it secret. Young people can be hurting themselves over long periods of time without ever telling friends or family. They hardly ever seek medical attention or support. Almost all self-harm is done in private, and on parts of the body that are not visible to others.

'People often link self-harm to suicide but for me it was something very different; it was my alternative to suicide; my way of coping even though sometimes I wished that my world would end!'

How does it start?

Many young people say that when they first harm themselves they believe it is a 'one-off' and that they won't do it again. But it doesn't solve the problems they are trying to cope with, and their difficult feelings soon come back again, leading them into a cycle of harming themselves to try to cope.

Some young people have told us that they started to self-harm by accident – when they injured themselves accidentally – and then started to cause themselves injuries on purpose to create the same feelings again.

Young people who self-harm usually feel very guilty and ashamed of what they do, and do not want to talk about it

---

Is it really addictive?

It is habit-forming, and some people believe you can become physically addicted to self-harm. There is evidence to show that chemicals, called 'endogenous opioids' are released when the body is injured in any way. They are pleasurable and can make you less sensitive to pain. However, self-harm is not simply about chasing physical pleasure or relief through artificially stimulating a 'natural' reaction – it has to be understood for what it means to the young person who does it. Often it is a way of coping or distracting yourself, that is habit-forming. In other words, young people get used to it, and come to rely on it.

How do young people feel about harming themselves?

Young people who self-harm usually feel very guilty and ashamed of what they do, and do not want to talk about it. The stigma associated with self-harm is unhelpful, and stops people getting the support and information they need to find better and more helpful ways of coping.

What are the signs that someone is self-harming?

It is very difficult to tell whether someone is self-harming. One sign might be that they insist on covering up their bodies – even when it is warm. They may avoid activities that involve showing themselves – such as swimming or games. Secretive behaviour, and wanting to be alone lots can also be a sign.

'People often link self-harm to suicide but for me it was something very different; it was my alternative to suicide'

Many of the usual signs of emotional distress – becoming withdrawn, quiet, appearing 'washed out' and lacking energy – can also be signs that someone is self-harming.

⇨ The above information is an extract from the National Inquiry into Self-harm among Young People's document 'The truth about self-harm – for young people and their friends and families' and is reprinted with permission. For more information, or to view the full document, please visit their website at www.selfharmuk.org

Hurting themselves

Information from Channel 4

By Claire Laurent

'Cutting myself is such a private thing. I find it hard to talk to other people about how I feel. They don't understand. They think I'm seeking attention – that's the last thing I want.'

Deliberate self-harm involves acts such as poisoning, over-dosing, cutting or head banging, causing some tissue damage to the body. The intention is to cause harm rather than to kill oneself although of course there is a danger that death could result from the act. It is considered to be a deliberate non-fatal act done in the knowledge that it could be fatal.

Self-harm is called many things – self-injury, self-abuse, parasuicide or self-mutilation. The latter expression is not often used because generally the aim of deliberate self-harm is not to maim the body. Self-harm tends to be repetitive. It's not about seeking sexual pleasure, body decoration or even being cool or part of a gang – although this can be a starting point for some who then find relief from the act and so repeat it.

How common is it?

'Cutting was always a very secret thing … You feel so ashamed, so bad about yourself. You feel no one will ever understand.'

Recent research of more than 1,000 15- to 21-year-olds commissioned by the Department of Health shows that more than 50% knew someone who had self-harmed. A study in the *British Journal of Psychiatry* in 1998 of teenagers presenting at Accident & Emergency departments for treatment for self-harm found that every hour three young people self-harm.

However, visits to hospital A & E departments for treatment by self-harming teenagers represent only the tip of the iceberg. A study published in the *BMJ* in November 2002 found that out of a study of 6,020 teenagers aged 15 and 16 years, 398 (6.9%) reported an act of deliberate self-harm in the previous year, although only 12.6% of these presented at hospital for treatment. The same study found that self-harm was four times more common amongst girls than boys.

Deliberate self-harm involves acts such as poisoning, overdosing, cutting or head banging, causing some tissue damage to the body

'Whether deliberate self-harm is becoming more common or whether it's simply more openly discussed than previously is not clear,' says Dr Rory O'Connor, health psychologist and a member of the suicidal behaviour research group at the University of Strathclyde. It's likely, however, that the figures don't include some who regularly self-harm but find ways to keep this to themselves, not seeking medical help and thereby putting themselves at further risk of scarring or infection.

Why self-harm?

'The feeling of wanting to hurt myself would build up. I could put off doing it for a while but I couldn't last forever. I knew I had to get help.'

Dr O'Connor says there are three main reasons why young people self-harm: 'It's a form of communication, a form of problem solving and a form of coping.

'You are trying to communicate intolerable psychological pain, feelings of not being able to cope or feelings of shame, which is common in those who have been abused. They want to make real their mental pain,' he says.

Dr O'Connor says: 'They have tried to solve their problems though other solutions and haven't been able to and they can't think of alternatives. Self-harm can bring them relief from their painful emotions and it is this that can make the act repetitive. They find relief from it and so repeat the act whenever life becomes too stressful to deal with.'

The risk factors
⇨ bullying
⇨ concerns about gender orientation
⇨ personal or family history of mental illness
⇨ personal or family history of self-harming behaviour
⇨ alcohol/substance misuse
⇨ feelings of apathy, anger or hopelessness
⇨ history of sexual abuse
⇨ promiscuous behaviour
⇨ copycat behaviour.

Copycats

'Young people copying others who self-harm can be a real problem,' says Dr O'Connor. 'There is a danger of it becoming a behaviour that defines a group and that's very worrying. If someone in the gang does it then others in the gang may do it too. It becomes the cool thing to do. The problem is what happens when you up the ante? If you do it once to copy and get a buzz or a rush out of it, a release, then irrespective of your motivation to do it the first time, do you increase the self-harm the next time?' In this way he says that youngsters might continue to self-harm with or without the peer pressure that started it off.

Warning signs

While cuts to the body or an overdose seem evidence enough, getting someone to talk about self-harm and to admit they might have a problem is not always easy. And of course, cuts and bruises can be covered up and excused so parents might not be aware their child has a problem.

'Parents need to look out for mood changes,' says Dr O'Connor. While he admits this isn't easy given your average teenager he says parents should watch for whether a young person is functioning fully: Are they sleeping properly? Are they eating? Are they still socialising and doing the things they usually enjoy?

Self-harm tends to be repetitive

He says parents need to keep lines of communication open and to listen to problems young people might voice. 'A crisis may look minor from the outside but the impact on a young person's wellbeing can be quite remarkable,' he says.

A government campaign in England called Read the Signs has been launched to encourage young people to recognise the signs of mental ill health and to try and tackle the stigma that still surrounds it.

Is there a risk of suicide?

A history of self-harm is one of the risk factors amongst people who go on to complete suicide. It is thought that the risk of dying through suicide is 100 times greater for those who self-harm than the general population (*British Journal of Psychiatry*, 1998).

Reducing the suicide rate is now a national health priority. About 5,000 people are thought to kill themselves every year – the majority of whom are young men – and the government is working hard through implementation of the National Service Framework for Mental Health to reduce this by at least one-fifth by 2010.

Dr O'Connor says that if you are concerned that someone you know might be contemplating suicide, ask them about it. 'You are not planting ideas into their heads,' he stresses. Also be aware if a young person:
⇨ talks or jokes about suicide
⇨ makes statements about being worthless or hopeless

⇨ is preoccupied with death – through reading, poetry, drawing or music
⇨ loses interest in things previously cared about
⇨ engages in risk-taking behaviour – walking in front of traffic, for example
⇨ is suddenly happier or calmer when there appears to be no resolution to their problems.

If you are concerned, try and establish how immediate the risk might be. If you think it's imminent, don't leave the person alone. Talk to them about their plans and don't minimise or dismiss their problems. Reassure them that it's possible to get help and feel better. Once an immediate risk appears to subside, book an appointment with their GP and go with them.

How to help

'What helped was having someone to talk to who was reliable and didn't rush me. I haven't done anything to myself for ages now. Sometimes I feel like it, but I don't need to do it any more, and the feeling goes.'

Most people who self-harm are unhappy about their behaviour and are likely to feel embarrassed or defensive if questioned about it. It's important to give young people the chance to talk, without criticising their self-harming behaviour.

'We should be training our young people in how to engage in positive mental health strategies,' says Dr O'Connor. 'They don't know how to cope with the changes and challenges of modern life.'

To do this young people need to know how to express their feelings in more appropriate ways and to be encouraged to find solutions other than self-harming. Going for a walk or playing sport can help channel anger,

while drawing or writing about how they feel can be relaxing. Dr O'Connor says it's important for parents to boost their child's self-esteem, giving verbal praise and helping them set achievable goals. He says parents need to check they're giving supportive messages and not creating unreasonable expectations for their children.

Treatment

The first port of call for treatment is likely to be your child's GP. He or she will refer them on to specialist mental health services such as a clinical psychologist or perhaps to the practice counsellor. However, you may find the school has a counsellor who is in touch with the sort of pressures your child faces and can help them deal with some of them, or the school may refer them to an educational psychologist. It depends, says Dr O'Connor, both on what's available and the cause of a young person's self-harm.

Cognitive behavioural therapy (CBT) may be useful to help a young person think positively and develop new and more positive ways of responding to stress.

Thanks are due to YoungMinds for permission to use quotations from their publications in this feature.

⇨ The above information is reprinted with kind permission from Channel 4. Visit www.channel4.com for more information.

© Channel 4

Talking to someone who understands is an important way of breaking the self-harm cycle

Talking about self-harm

Information from the National Inquiry into Self-harm among Young People

Why do people self-harm in secret? Why don't they ask for help?

When we asked young people who have self-harmed what stopped them from seeking help, they often said that at first they thought the behaviour was a 'one off', and it was only after a few times that they found they couldn't stop.

But one of the biggest fears young people told us about, and the biggest obstacle to getting help, was the fear that self-harm, the only coping strategy that had been keeping them going, might be taken away from them.

They also said that they thought they could cope on their own, or that they were planning to sort things out and didn't need any help.

Many young people were worried about what others would think of them, when they found out they were hurting themselves intentionally. They were also worried that they would not be taken seriously. Many feared that no one would understand why they had done it, or would be able to help them. Girls were particularly sensitive about being labelled or dismissed as being an 'attention seeker' or 'stupid' if they asked for help.

Most young people felt that they would not self-harm again, and they wanted to put the fact that they had done it to the back of their minds. Boys in particular felt that the situation and their injuries were not serious enough to ask for help. Very few young people understood at the beginning that things might change for the worse again, and that they could come to depend on harming themselves to cope with their lives.

Many young people said they did not have anyone they felt they could talk to apart, sometimes, from close friends. They certainly didn't know how to contact support services. Some were worried that if they were open about their self-harm, this could affect their choices for the future:

Young people and **Self Harm** *a National Inquiry*

they were worried they wouldn't be able to work in professions such as teaching, nursing, or childcare because of perceptions that people who self-harm are 'dangerous' and should not be allowed to work with children.

Young people also told us they were worried that their secret would become 'public property' and that they would lose control over the situation and who knew about it, once they told someone else.

Should I tell someone that I am harming myself?

Yes, because this is often the first step to getting out of the cycle.

It isn't always simple or easy, and could be one of the most difficult – but most important – things you do. Young people have told us that the reaction they got when they first told someone about their self-harm was very important in deciding whether or not they looked for and got further help.

While some young people have experienced negative attitudes when they have told someone, it is possible to get good support from people who understand self-harm, or who care about you and your feelings, not just the behaviour itself.

If you are worried about the person you tell sharing the information with others, you can choose to tell a health professional like a doctor or a nurse to start with, or a counsellor. You can also telephone a helpline. These people have a duty to keep it to themselves while you get used to the idea of telling others. They can

offer you help and advice while you prepare.

Unfortunately, some young people told us that they felt forced into discussing their self-harm, for example by teachers or health professionals who had guessed what was going on. Some young people felt very distressed by the idea that these workers would tell others – like fellow teachers or their parents. If this happens to you, you could try explaining that self-harm is a coping mechanism and not the same as suicidal behaviour.

You can ask them what will happen next, once you have told them, and who else they plan to tell or involve. You can ask them not to tell particular people. You can even ask them not to tell anyone at all, although this can be very difficult for the other person, and it can mean you do not get all of the help and support that you need.

> *'The one thing that always helps if I'm feeling really bad is to be around someone that I trust. I may look bad and not be very talkative – but just being around someone who doesn't question my odd behaviour and lets me be around them without talking or expectations helps.'*

What is the best way to tell someone that I have harmed myself?

It can be a very worrying decision, and it can be hard to decide who to tell and how to tell them. Telling someone about your self-harm shows strength and courage. But it can often be a huge relief to be able to let go of such a secret, or at least share it.

The most important thing of all is that you feel comfortable with who you decide to tell, what you tell them, when and where. Don't feel pressured into answering questions or saying more than you want to. You can set the pace. Remember, if you want to tell a professional or family member, you can take a friend with you to support you.

There are many ways of telling people and there are no rules about how it should be done. You can speak to someone, write to or email them, or even just show them your injuries or scars and let that pave the way to talking about it. If you tell someone in writing, think about taking some time to talk to them afterwards, as well.

It is very important, if you can, to try to focus on the feelings or situation that led you to start harming yourself, rather than on the behaviour itself. This can help people feel less bewildered about why you might be doing it.

Revealing self-harm to someone can bring out a wide range of feelings in them, both positive and negative. The person you tell may need some time to get used to what you have told them and think about their response, so try to give this to them. They may well be able to respond more positively after some time has passed and they have had the chance to think over what you have said. It can be helpful to them to know why you are telling them – whether you just want to let go of a secret you have carried on your own, or you would like their help or advice.

As hard as telling someone may be for you, it may also be very hard for the person you choose to tell – especially if it is someone close to you. They may need to get support for themselves, both before and after talking about it with you.

Try to be prepared for the fact that sometimes your situation can feel worse immediately after telling someone. But once you are over this hurdle, there is usually support available to help you recover – even if the support is through friends or family.

Who can I tell?

A major factor in how the person you tell responds will be the kind of relationship they have with you, and how well they know you. A parent who might feel they are very close to you may be more shocked, for example, than a nurse.

Most people (no matter who they are, a friend, a parent, a teacher or a professional) don't really understand self-harm, and it's hard to predict how someone will react when you tell them. Try to keep in mind that they may have a range of feelings, and one of them will most likely be shock.

Young people have told us that the people they have been able to talk to included:
- ⇨ Friends – young people said they were far more likely to talk it over with friends their own age than anyone else.
- ⇨ Family members.
- ⇨ Someone at school but not necessarily a teacher you know well.
- ⇨ Telephone help lines were also mentioned.
- ⇨ Internet support: not many people had looked for help on the internet, but there are some useful sources online.
- ⇨ A doctor or nurse.

Some young people have said that the reaction they got when talking to health workers was unhelpful. In this case you can always seek further help. Many GPs and nurses will be sympathetic, and know how to help and no one should be put off from seeking help because of negative attitudes.

'Many people stop hurting themselves when the time is right for them. Everyone is different and if they feel the need to self-harm at the moment, they shouldn't feel guilty about it – it is a way of surviving, and doing it now does NOT mean that they will need to do it forever. It is a huge step towards stopping when they begin to talk about it, because it means that they are starting to think about what might take its place eventually.'

What if someone tells me they are self-harming?

The reaction a young person receives when they disclose their self-harm has a major impact on whether they go on to get help and recover. What young people who self-harm need is understanding, care and concern for their injuries, time and support as well as encouragement to talk about the underlying feelings or situations that have led them to harm themselves. Getting angry, shouting, or accusing them is likely to aggravate the situation.

Young people who have self-harmed want responses that are non-judgemental, caring and respectful. It's very important to see the person, and the reasons they have harmed themselves, and not just to focus on

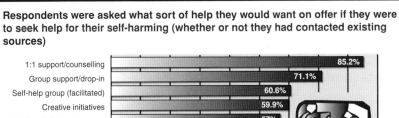

What young people thought would be helpful

Respondents were asked what sort of help they would want on offer if they were to seek help for their self-harming (whether or not they had contacted existing sources)

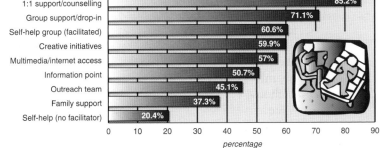

	percentage
1:1 support/counselling	85.2%
Group support/drop-in	71.1%
Self-help group (facilitated)	60.6%
Creative initiatives	59.9%
Multimedia/internet access	57%
Information point	50.7%
Outreach team	45.1%
Family support	37.3%
Self-help (no facilitator)	20.4%

Notes: people who visited the National Inquiry into Self-Harm's website were asked to fill in a detailed multiple choice questionnaire. A total of 142 young people aged from 13 upwards, with an average age of 20, completed questionnaires. There were 137 females and five males.
Source: The National Inquiry into Self-harm, 'Truth Hurts' report, 2006.

the harm itself. It's also important to allow the young person to take the discussion at their own pace.

Most importantly, you should try to hear about self-harm without panic, revulsion or condemnation. This can be hard as it's difficult to understand, but remember, it is quite common, and it's usually used as a way of coping by young people.

One of the biggest fears young people told us about was the fear that self-harm, the only coping strategy that had been keeping them going, might be taken away from them

---

If you are a friend of the person who is self-harming, you might have some of the same reactions that a parent would – disbelief, fear for your friend, worry about what to do for the best. The person may tell you but want you to keep it a secret. This can leave you feeling distressed and isolated, with no one to talk to yourself.

Working out what to do, or trying to decide how much danger your friend is in, is not easy. It may be helpful, if you are a young person, to find someone older that you trust and believe you can confide in.

Occasionally, someone may reveal to you that they have harmed themselves immediately after they have injured themselves – perhaps more than they meant to. They may be worried that they have done lasting damage. If this happens it is best to see that their injuries are attended to and they have time to recover from any physical trauma before exploring the reasons behind it.

What if I discover my son or daughter or someone I care for is self-harming?

⇨ Try to be accepting and open-minded. Let the person know you are there for them, and reassure them that they are loved. Assure them that it's okay to talk about their need to self-harm, and reassure them that they have your support even if you don't understand why they are doing it or what they are going through.

⇨ Offer to lend a hand in getting them professional help; from a GP, counsellor, therapist, or community psychiatric nurse. But try to avoid taking control- many people who self-harm feel it is an important way of having some control over their lives. Try to not to take it too personally if your son or daughter cannot talk to you because you are too close.

⇨ Avoid giving ultimatums; for example, 'stop or else...' as they rarely work, and may well drive the behaviour underground, and you might not get any further chances to discuss the topic and really deal with it. Self-harm can be very addictive, and if a person feels the need to do it,

they will normally find a way. It is important that the decision to stop comes from the person who is self-harming.

⇨ Find out more. There are a growing number of useful books on the topic of self-harm, as well as some informative websites. Educating yourself on the subject can go a long way towards helping you be understanding and supportive.

⇨ Try to sort out your own feelings. Be honest with yourself about how your daughter or son's self-harm is affecting you. It's not unusual to feel hurt, devastated, shocked, angry, sad, frightened, guilty, responsible, hopeless, or powerless. It's not easy knowing that a loved one is hurting him or herself, and it might be worth considering seeing a counsellor or therapist for yourself if you are struggling to cope with strong emotions or feel in need of support.

Remember, finding out that someone is self-harming is a real opportunity to help them deal with many other problems they are having.

⇨ The above information is an extract from the National Inquiry into Self-harm among Young People's document 'The truth about self-harm – for young people and their friends and families' and is reprinted with permission. For more information, or to view the full document, please visit their website at www.selfharmuk.org

© *Camelot Foundation and the Mental Health Foundation*

My self-harm story

21-year-old Laura has been self-harming for two years. Here she shares her story

I started self-harming about two years ago. I had an argument with my flatmate and this set it off. It wasn't a serious row; it was quite a silly one to be honest. However, I think this triggered off a lot of my self-esteem issues. I had a really hard time at school and was bullied a lot and I ended up finding it hard to get close to people. My feelings of self-worth vanished again after the argument and in order to combat this I started to cut myself. Not seriously at first; surface marks more than anything else. The only person I told was my boyfriend at the time and the only reason I told him was because I didn't want him to actually see the cuts and then worry. However, he did worry. Immensely.

> **'Self-harm, in my opinion, was not about dying or trying to kill yourself, it was about feeling alive; if I felt a bit of pain then I knew that I existed'**

My main method of self-harm was cutting, although I'm quite a clumsy person and I knew how easily I bruised so I used to hit my hand against the wall too. This was nowhere near as effective as cutting. At one stage it got so serious that during the uni holidays when I was working I would cut before going to work, at lunchtime and then before going to bed. Sometimes I would do it more than three times a day. I was also quite obsessed with how deep the cuts were. The worse I felt, the deeper they had to be. Sometimes if they weren't deep enough then I would go over them again. I cut my legs because they were the easiest places to hide them. If things got bad and I couldn't wait until I actually took my trousers off then I would cut my arm but wear long sleeves until they healed.

The act of self-harm

My preferred weapon was a razor blade. I would buy cheap razors and break them up so that I would get the blade out. I also had a wee Stanley knife that I carried with me at all times so that I would feel secure and safe. I knew that if I had it then nothing could hurt me.

Immediately before I self-harmed I would feel numb, completely numb. The whole point of cutting was to actually try and be aware of something again because it often seemed like I didn't actually feel anything. It was quite a weird sensation. Sometimes I also felt quite detached. At times it was as if I was actually watching myself live my life, as if I was watching a film, I didn't actually feel real and nothing around me did either.

When I was cutting I never cared about how much damage I inflicted on myself. The more the better. However, I was always careful to avoid veins and arteries. Self-harm, in my opinion, was not about dying or trying to kill yourself, it was about feeling alive; if I felt a bit of pain then I knew that I existed. During my dark times the cutting never inflicted any pain. I was numb to it all but I wanted to feel – that was the whole point.

Whenever I cut, all I could think about was the anguish inside me.

Straight afterwards I always felt relieved. I felt as if I could face living again, I could cope with any silly little problem like not knowing what I could have for dinner or that I had missed the bus. It made me feel 'real' again.

Later I always felt embarrassed about it. I used to do my utmost to try and hide it from others; if this meant wearing jumpers in the summer then that's what I did. I never wore a skirt that would reveal anything. It is only now, two years after I first cut myself that I actually feel comfortable wearing anything that may show some of my scars. The embarrassment was horrible as I felt completely alone and isolated. I never realised how common it actually was.

Alone

I pushed so many people away from me. I used to hide in my room and wait for the flat to empty before I would even consider making food or even go to the bathroom.

I avoided phone calls. I always pretended I wasn't in. If I saw someone I knew on the street then I would cross the road so that I wouldn't have to speak to them.

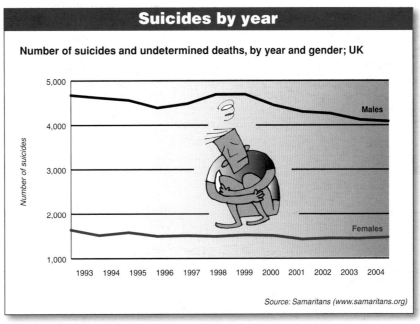

Suicides by year

Number of suicides and undetermined deaths, by year and gender; UK

Males

Females

Number of suicides — 5,000 / 4,000 / 3,000 / 2,000 / 1,000

1993 1994 1995 1996 1997 1998 1999 2000 2001 2002 2003 2004

Source: Samaritans (www.samaritans.org)

I became lost in my own world of destruction.

Getting help

My ex-boyfriend was the only person who knew about it all and he helped me immensely. He encouraged me to seek help. I ended up at the doctor's and I had the most fantastic GP ever. She was really nice but she could see right through the front I would put on for her. I very rarely showed any sign of weakness in front of other people. If I met anyone in the street I was always 'bouncy, happy go lucky Laura without a care in the world'. She diagnosed me as depressed and put me on Fluoxetine (i.e. Prozac).

'People look down on self-harm a lot and just fob it off as attention seeking. However, a lot of self-harmers cut/burn/whatever in private. They don't do it for attention'

My doctor referred me to a counsellor who, in my opinion, didn't really help. I only went to two sessions. I found it really difficult to talk to people about this. After that I convinced myself I was better and stopped going to see the doctor and I stopped taking my antidepressants. Then things went bad again and I attempted to kill myself. I ended up in A&E and I ran away from the hospital and was nearly sectioned. I was then sent to a psychiatrist who helped me a lot. He was a lovely man and made me feel really comfortable and he was easy to talk to, unlike the counsellor.

Talking about it

I became more open about it all and now people do know about my self-harm. It was a hard step to take because it forced me to accept I had a problem. All my friends have been fantastic and they have all offered to help me. The best form of support that they can give me is the knowledge that they are there for me. The friends that have tried to push their active support onto me are no longer my friends, because I pushed their support away so much that they took offence. I found it extremely difficult when people were forcing their help onto me and were forcing me to try and accept their opinions and suggestions. Deep down I know that they were just looking out for me but I resented that.

Distraction

The best distraction that has helped me is diversion. If I feel the need to cut now then I leave my flat. I will go and sit in the park or go to a church and sit there or even go to the cinema. This way I am not likely to cut because I will only do it in the privacy of my own flat, whether it is in the bathroom or my bedroom.

Now

I do not harm as much any more. I can go three months without cutting but every so often I feel the need and I cannot get rid of the urge. Recently I did cut because I didn't know what else to do. I get angry with the media cover of self-harm. There are a lot of people who cut because it is seen as cool because celebrities like Marilyn Manson do it. However, there are a lot of people who actually do it because they need to feel a release. They are angry or hurting and don't know how else to release the tension that is building up inside.

People who self-harm may cut themselves with knives or razors

There are so many people who do it because it is cool and there is not enough support for the rest of the people who do it for real reasons. People look down on self-harm a lot and just fob it off as attention seeking. However, a lot of self-harmers cut/burn/whatever in private. They don't do it for attention. They don't tell the world that they do it; they self-harm because there is no other way out for them. That was how it was for me.

⇨ The above information is reprinted with kind permission from TheSite.org. Visit www.thesite.org for more information.

© TheSite.org

Truth hurts

Report of the National Inquiry into Self-harm among Young People – executive summary

Introduction

Self-harm among young people is a major public health issue in the UK. It affects at least one in 15 young people and some evidence suggests that rates of self-harm in the UK are higher than anywhere else in Europe. Self-harm blights the lives of young people and seriously affects their relationships with families and friends. It presents a major challenge to all those in services and organisations that work with young people, from schools through to hospital accident and emergency departments.

Self-harm among young people is a major public health issue in the UK

Levels of self-harm are one indicator of the mental health and mental well-being of young people in our society in general. Recently there has been a shift in government strategies, across the UK, towards recognising and promoting better mental health and emotional well-being for all children and young people. These initiatives may eventually do a great deal to reduce self-harm among young people but the Inquiry found that implementation to date is patchy and there is not yet an adequate evidence base specific to self-harm.

This Inquiry set out to try and find the definitive answers to the key questions:
⇨ what is self-harm
⇨ how common is it among young people
⇨ can it be prevented
⇨ how can we respond better to young people who self-harm.

Self-harm describes a wide range of things that people do to themselves in a deliberate and usually hidden way. In the vast majority of cases self-harm remains a secretive behaviour that can go on for a long time without being discovered. Self-harm can involve:
⇨ cutting
⇨ burning
⇨ scalding
⇨ banging or scratching one's own body
⇨ breaking bones
⇨ hair pulling
⇨ ingesting toxic substances or objects.

Young people who self-harm mainly do so because they have no other way of coping with problems and emotional distress in their lives. This can be to do with factors ranging from bullying to family breakdown. But self-harm is not a good way of dealing with such problems. It provides only temporary relief and does not deal with the underlying issues.

Although some very young children are known to self-harm, and some adults too, the Inquiry focused on young people aged between 11 and 25 years because rates of self-harm are much higher among young people, and the average age of onset is 12 years old.

The issue

There is relatively little research or other data on the prevalence of self-harm among young people in the UK or on the reasons why young people self-harm. It became clear to the Inquiry that self-harm is a symptom rather than the core problem. It masks underlying emotional and psychological trauma and a successful strategy for responding to self-harm must be based on this fundamental understanding.

The evidence about reasons why young people self-harm shows that there are a wide range of factors that might contribute. Young people told the Inquiry that there are often multiple triggers for their self-harm, often daily stresses rather than significant changes or events. These include things like feeling isolated, academic pressures, suicide or self-

harm by someone close to them, and low self-esteem or poor body image which can make them feel unstable and even hate themselves. Many described how self-harm gets out 'all the hurt, anger and pain' but that relief is so short-lived they do it many times. Crucially young people talked about having no alternatives: 'I don't know how to release my feelings in any other way'. Many also explained that their self-harm is about feeling dead inside and that self-harm 'brought them back to life' and made them feel 'something – alive and real'. Because young people often find release or even positives from self-harm it can be difficult to envisage coping with life without it: 'I have found the decision to stop harming myself infinitely more difficult than the decision to start.'

Prevention

School-based work appears to be one of the most promising areas where the prevention of self-harm can be successfully tackled. One of the key findings of the Inquiry, which is backed up by previous research, is that many young people prefer to turn to other young people for support. Young people told the Inquiry that often all they want is to be able to talk to someone who will listen and respect them, not specifically about self-harm but about problems and issues in their daily lives. Many said that had this been available to them they may never have started to self-harm. 'If there had been people to talk to at school then maybe I wouldn't have felt the need to start self-harming then.'

A number of schools have started to implement peer support schemes and all schools are now required by the Department for Education and Skills to have anti-bullying strategies. The Inquiry found evidence which shows that these are significantly more effective when they are part of a whole school approach to good mental health for all.

A key factor that many young people told the Inquiry exacerbates their self-harm is social isolation. Many young people told the Inquiry that it helps tremendously to know that they are not the only young person in the world who has problems in day-to-day life and deals with these through self-harm. We were told that the feeling of being alone is hard enough but reaching out is even harder: 'As someone who had self-harmed I found it hard to accept that I wasn't alone as I'd never heard of it – I wanted someone else to clarify what I did, show that they understood and be willing to listen and not judge.'

Young people who self-harm can find it very hard to talk about it and are often afraid of how people will react

---

Disclosure and immediate response

It was clear to the Inquiry that young people who self-harm can find it hard to talk about it and are often afraid of how people will react. 'At school my self-harm was treated very badly. It was treated as a piece of gossip throughout the staff and the head teacher asked me to leave as a result, saying that I was a lovely person but he couldn't have it in his school.' The reaction a young person receives when they disclose their self-harm can have a critical influence on whether they go on to access supportive services. It can be also hard for family, friends, and professionals to handle a young person's disclosure of self-harm.

The key message from young people is that they need preventative measures that are non-judgemental and respectful. Equally importantly, school staff and others must reach out to young people – rather than expect young people to come forward – and provide opportunities for them to discuss problems before they turn to self-harm as a way of coping.

The Inquiry was told that for many young people disclosure of their self-harm was a very bad experience. They told us that they lost control of who else would be told (e.g. parents, other services) and that attitudes changed unhelpfully. 'My doctor looked at me differently once I told her why I was there. It was as if I were being annoying and wasting her time.'

A strong theme in the evidence presented to the Inquiry was the need for school staff and others who work with young people to have a much better awareness and understanding of self-harm. This includes a basic understanding of what self-harm is, why young people do it, how to respond appropriately, and what other support and services are available. This alone would make it more likely that young people who self-harm get the help that they need.

Support and therapeutic interventions

The Inquiry heard about a wide range of services for young people who self-harm, across the UK. Young people appear to benefit very much from some of these approaches, although to date there is not a strong evidence base to demonstrate their effectiveness. The Inquiry concluded that more comprehensive and targeted research is needed in order to shape the development of effective services, support and therapeutic interventions. A key message from young people is that they want a range of options, a one-size-fits-all approach will not work. 'I tried so many – I found it hard to adapt to something different, when I was used to coping with my own way. Eventually though I found a way of coping which I got on with and it helped me to stop.'

The Inquiry heard from young people that self-help was critical. They stressed the crucial importance of being able to distract themselves from self-harm even for a short period of time. For some distraction can be a first step towards tackling their self-harm and it should be treated as a positive step. Successful distraction techniques that young people told the Inquiry about included using a red water-soluble felt tip pen to mark – or rubbing ice – instead of cutting, hitting a punch bag to vent anger and frustration, and flicking elastic bands on the wrist. 'I tried holding an ice-cube, elastic band flicking on the wrist, writing down my thoughts, hitting a pillow, listening to music, writing down pros and cons – but the most helpful to my recovery was the five minutes rule, where if you feel like you want to self-harm you wait for five minutes before you do, then see if you can go another five minutes, and so on till eventually the urge is over.'

Recovery

The Inquiry recognised the need to clarify what is meant by recovery in terms of self-harm. Some young people interpret it as reducing their self-harm as they tackle the underlying issues, using distraction techniques and minimising the damage that self-harm inflicts; others interpret it as completely stopping self-harm. Professionals in particular need to be clear that many young people use this first interpretation.

Some young people find that over time, their needs or circumstances have changed to the point where they do not feel that they need to self-harm. Others manage to learn new coping strategies for dealing with difficult emotions or circumstances, often by adopting successful distraction techniques which help them cope with the immediate urge to self-harm. This may involve some degree of self-harm, at least at the beginning. Recovery is often a long, slow process and involves changing the circumstances which caused the young person to self-harm in the first place. There is no 'quick fix'.

Self-harm is a symptom rather than the core problem. It masks underlying emotional trauma

---

Conclusion

The research, personal testimony and expert opinion submitted to the Inquiry has demonstrated how far-reaching the issue of self-harm is for young people. The guilt and secrecy associated with self-harm impacts on their daily lives: their relationships; the clothes they wear; their interactions with their friends; and their sense of self-worth. If and when they do tell someone else about their self-harm, the whole issue is frequently taken completely out of their hands, and their previously secretive behaviour becomes common knowledge. They are aware that everyone is watching them closely in case they self-harm again. Most importantly, the focus very often remains on the self-harm, not the underlying causes, which means that they feel they have no other option but to continue to self-harm.

Self-harm among young people is a serious public health challenge that everyone in contact with young people must rise to. However, we should be encouraged by the clear direction set out by the young people who contributed to the Inquiry. They have mapped out the way that we should understand self-harm and how everyone involved with young people can work towards prevention and better responses to it. Equally encouragingly the Inquiry has heard evidence about a wide range of services and interventions, many of which hold great promise in tackling this hidden epidemic.
March 2006

⇨ The above information is an extract from the National Inquiry into Self-harm among Young People's document 'Truth hurts – Report of the National Inquiry into Self-harm among Young People' and is reprinted with permission. For more information, or to view the full report, please visit their website at www.selfharmuk.org
© Camelot Foundation and the Mental Health Foundation

Self-harm and Scotland's older people

Self-harm – the secret epidemic that is afflicting Scotland's older people

A hidden epidemic of self-harm among older people exists in Scotland, with thousands of cases admitted to hospital each year and many more covering up their injuries, mental health campaigners have warned.

Support groups for people who self-harm report growing numbers of cases emerging among people in their 40s, 50s and 60s.

The scale of self-harm in older people is unknown because they are much less likely to come forward for help because of the stigma around mental health issues. But campaign groups believe it may be just as big a problem as self-harm among teenagers – the group usually associated with cutting, burning and hurting themselves to deal with their feelings.

Figures suggest there are between 14,000 and 16,000 admissions a year to hospitals in Scotland as a result of self-harm.

Three-quarters of these are under-45s, the vast majority of them teenagers. About 3,000 admissions are among older people, but it is believed many more may be self-harming but have become better at covering it up and coping with their injuries themselves.

Patrick Little, of the mental health organisation Penumbra, which runs projects across Scotland, said it no longer only worked with youngsters self-harming.

'One of our projects works with people aged 18 and upwards and we are working with 60-year-olds who have lived their lives in pain,' he said.

'They will have started when they were young and lived their lives self-harming. I would say this is not as uncommon as people think. I have been saying that maybe we need to start looking at self-harm in the elderly because it's an issue that is there.'

By Lyndsay Moss, Health Correspondent

Mr Little said a lot of people's first experience of serious pain may be when they become elderly and lose their partner or when their own health starts to fail.

'I have no doubt that if you started to dig there you would start to uncover new self-harm among elderly people,' he said. 'People who are not young and self-harm often feel more ostracised because it is felt that this is a young people's issue and they shouldn't be doing this.

'Our understanding is that if this is a response to emotional pain it shouldn't matter what age you are.'

Mr Little said it was estimated that only around one in ten incidents of self-harm resulted in someone going to hospital.

Linda Dunion, campaign director for the Scottish mental health group See Me, said self-harm among older people was a particular concern because it remained hidden.

'It is something that has come to our attention recently. Because it is so associated with young people the general public don't actually realise that it does affect older people as well,' she said. 'Self-harm in older people is probably underestimated. It tends to be really hard for older people to come forward and get help.

'It is such a hidden problem that we are only now beginning to question how many older people may be involved. If they are not going for help they are not being counted.'

Lindsay Scott, of Help the Aged Scotland, said older people had to deal with difficult issues which could lead to mental health problems and self-harm.

'With the breakdown of the family unit, more and more older people are finding themselves in a state not just of poverty but also of isolation and neglect,' she said.

'An isolated pensioner who has no one to talk to, very little money and the worry of bills to pay could find themselves pushed into a corner.'

A Scottish Executive spokeswoman said: 'We are aware that self-harm can be an indicator of mental ill health.

'We have a range of measures in place to improve mental health and wellbeing for all and one priority area is to improve mental health and wellbeing in later life.'

'At 41 you are meant to be in control'

Karen Martin began self-harming in her twenties. Now 41, she is still struggling to deal with the cutting and scratching that has become part of her identity.

She said the stigma of being an older self-harmer meant many in their 40s, 50s and 60s were unlikely to seek help.

'It makes me feel numb and is a way of controlling my emotions.

'But that feeling may only last a few minutes and then I either have to cut myself again or distract myself.'

Ms Martin's self-harm came to a peak about six years ago when she was in an abusive relationship.

'My self-esteem was rock bottom. The only way to control my anger was to let it out by cutting.

'People think when you get to my age you are supposed to be in control of yourself and you shouldn't be resorting to this type of behaviour.

'But it's not an attention-seeking act. It's a controlling mechanism when something else in my life is out of control.'

8 August 2006

© *Scotsman*

Stop self-harming

It may seem as though you are all alone in the world; that there isn't anybody who can help you through your situation, but there is. Many organisations and groups can offer you support and there are also different strategies you can use to stop self-harming. Read on to find out more

'At the time that you are doing it, it may seem hard to stop self-harming, but if you keep working on it and get the help that you need, you will be able to. The best way is to get better coping skills in how to handle your usual stresses and triggers. Yes, you may have some relapses, I have had many, but all you can do then is to keep trying and trying and not give up,' Abbey.

Step 1: Be ready to take the first step

Accept that you are a self-harmer and you want to get out of this situation. Believe that you need to stop self-harming and you want to find a safer way of coping with your problems. Be brave, take a deep breath and seek some help. It has to be your decision, if you try to quit for anyone other than yourself you probably won't be able to stop.

Step 2: Talk to someone

The best way you can help yourself is by talking about how you feel and learning to deal with those issues that have caused you to self-harm in the first place. You may find you can turn to a close friend, family member or teacher. It may be that the anonymity of online discussion boards (such as the ones on TheSite) will help you start to talk about your issues and get the confidence to go on and find more professional help.

Step 3: Find distractions that work for you and develop better coping methods

⇨ Understand why you self-harm, what are your triggers?

⇨ Write down who you are angry at rather than taking that anger out on yourself. Pretend a pillow is that person and take your anger out on that instead.

⇨ Learn to recognise the patterns of your self-harming and find ways to distract yourself before the urge to hurt yourself becomes too great.

TheSite.org

⇨ Find other ways to cope with stresses.

⇨ Many people find counselling sessions or cognitive behavioural therapy useful. A trip to your GP can also open up other possibilities appropriate for you such as visiting a psychiatrist, or starting a course of antidepressants.

'The best way [to stop self-harming] is to get better coping skills'

⇨ You may find that being part of self-help group can also help, as it allows you to discuss your feelings with others in a similar situation. There are some useful resources on the internet on where you can find a support group in your area.

Step 4: Keep on keeping on

Stay with it, if you find that counselling/medication isn't working for you then re-evaluate your options and try another. Stay determined.

What stopped other self-harmers?

'I was afraid that if I would keep doing it that I might cut too deep one time and I would bleed to death.' – Abbey

'My mood lifted for a while, and I simply stopped having the desire to do it. Now I am tempted again, but it seems too much trouble to start dismantling the razor blades to use them, though I think that one time I will be so down that it won't. I have a little theory that there's no such thing as an ex-self-harmer, just as there's no such thing as an ex-alcoholic or junkie. It's more an on-going battle than one with an end. Though it is something that can be beaten, slipping back now and again is not something to be ashamed and disgusted of.' – David

⇨ The above information is reprinted with kind permission from TheSite.org. Visit www.thesite.org for more information.

© TheSite.org

Dear diary, I am harming myself less ... but I am a bit worried about my pillow ...

Minimising self-harm damage

Self-harmers often find the urge to hurt themselves uncontrollable. This article will help you minimise the damage you cause and know what to do if you or someone you know inflicts a serious injury

When you have the urge to self-injure try distractions first, self-harm really should be your last resort.

Distract yourself

The best initial method of preventing yourself from self-harming is distraction. Here are some distraction methods that have worked for TheSite users:

⇨ Concentrating on something happy in the future, such as a holiday;

⇨ Good friends, good times, laughter;

When you have the urge to self-injure try distractions first, self-harm really should be your last resort

---

⇨ Writing in a journal;
⇨ Listening to music;
⇨ Beating the living daylights out of pillows or cushions;
⇨ Screaming and shouting;
⇨ Exercise;
⇨ Alternate harming techniques that don't leave a mark such as holding ice cubes in the crook of the elbow, or drawing on the skin where you'd usually cut with red pen;
⇨ Having a bath;
⇨ Phoning a friend;
⇨ Writing a diary.

If you are going to harm yourself

⇨ Avoid drugs and alcohol as these can make you do more damage than you intended.

TheSite.org

⇨ Get your tetanus vaccination up to date. Check with your GP.
⇨ Try to avoid doing it when in hysterics as you may cause more damage than you intended.
⇨ Know basic first aid.

1. Cuts

Do:
⇨ Use new blades each time, or at the very least make sure they are clean;
⇨ Always clean your cuts using antiseptic;
⇨ Stay away from your wrists;
⇨ Use Vitamin E or some kind of scar-reducing cream to help minimise the scars;
⇨ Learn better coping skills (through therapy or otherwise) on how to handle the urges to cut.

Don't:
⇨ Cut too deep;
⇨ Clean up with tissue/cotton wool – use a sterile wipe.

First aid:
Small cuts
If you cut yourself use something clean to reduce the risk of infection. Avoid areas where there are large veins/arteries. Wash and apply a sterile dressing.

Large cuts and abrasions
⇨ Look for embedded objects, such as broken glass, but do not remove them as they could be preventing more severe blood loss, leave them for the doctor or nurse to sort out;
⇨ Apply a sterile dressing and direct pressure;
⇨ Elevate the area if possible;
⇨ If the bleeding is serious call 999;
⇨ If bleeding continues apply new dressings on top of the old ones;
⇨ Avoid using antiseptic creams/ lotions;
⇨ Seek medical help for deep cuts, keep the wound elevated and apply pressure;

⇨ Shock may occur if you lose a lot of blood or if you have severe burns. Seek medical help/ call an ambulance if necessary.

Alternate harming techniques that don't leave a mark include holding ice cubes in the crook of the elbow, or drawing on the skin where you'd usually cut with red pen

---

Is my cut infected?
If it is the outside area of the cut/gash will be hot, swollen and hard. It may have pus leaking and you may have a temperature. Seek medical help.

Holding ice cubes in the crook of the elbow can be an alternate harming technique

2. Burns and scalds
⇨ Cool any burn under cold running water for 10-15 minutes;
⇨ Dress the affected area with clean sterile non-fluffy material;
⇨ If the burn is larger than a 50 pence coin or runs deep into the skin seek medical attention;
⇨ Do not apply: lotions, creams, ointments, adhesive dressings, cotton wool;
⇨ Don't break any blisters.

3. Poisoning (drugs overdose etc.)
⇨ If you have poisoned yourself notify someone straight away;
⇨ If you find someone else who you suspect has poisoned themselves place the casualty in recovery position and call for help (999);
⇨ Monitor airway breathing and circulation;
⇨ Don't try and induce vomiting.

Further help
In an emergency call 999 and ask for ambulance services, or go straight to the nearest hospital's Accident and Emergency department. A&E departments may have a 'psychiatric liaison nurse' available during office hours for people attending A&E with self-injury. Other departments may also have 'deliberate self-harm' social workers as a part of their service. These professionals may offer a few counselling sessions or referrals. If you wish to see one of these, inform the triage nurse when you arrive at A&E.

If you feel the situation is less serious go to see your GP or call NHS Direct.

⇨ The above information is reprinted with kind permission from TheSite.org. If you would like more information, please visit www. thesite.org

© TheSite.org

Health professionals 'misunderstand self-harm'

Inquiry finds young people turn to friends for support

The government should launch a nationwide initiative to develop improved responses to young people who self-harm, an influential inquiry team has said.

The National Inquiry into Self-harm, funded by the Mental Health Foundation and the Camelot Foundation, says in its final report that there is little information available to help parents and professionals deal with youngsters who self-harm.

It suggests there are widespread misunderstandings among professionals and relatives that prevent young people from getting support and seeking help. Many turn to friends their own age rather than ask for assistance from adults who, if they are asked for help, often react inappropriately.

The report, *Truth hurts*, says that many young people often hurt themselves for long periods without ever disclosing their self-harm. If adults are told, they tend to focus on the self-harming behaviour rather than on the underlying causes, which often include bullying at school, poor relationships with parents, and problems associated with sexuality.

The inquiry also found that health, education and social care professionals are not receiving the guidance or formal training they need to support young people who self-harm.

Catherine McLoughlin, who chaired the inquiry, said: 'It is vital that everyone who comes into contact with young people has a basic understanding of what self-harm is, why people do it, and how to respond appropriately. At the very least they should avoid being judgemental towards young people who disclose self-harm, should treat them with care and respect and should acknowledge the emotional distress they are clearly experiencing.'

The chief executive of the Mental Health Foundation, Andrew McColloch, added: 'Self-harm is evidently a symptom of mental and emotional distress. We need to look past the behaviour and provide understanding, support and effective services for young people in the UK.'

Copies of *Truth hurts* are available from the National Inquiry's website.
12 April 2006

⇨ The above information is reprinted with kind permission from the Royal College of Nursing. Visit www.rcn.org.uk for more information.
© Royal College of Nursing

Self-harm and suicide

Information from Samaritans

Overview

Self-harm encompasses a wide variety of behaviours and acts; different terms such as attempted suicide or parasuicide may also be used to describe it. These acts involve differing degrees of risk to life, and differing degrees of suicidal intent, but all speak of intense emotional distress in the person who deliberately harms themselves.

People who have self-harmed are at greatly increased risk of suicide and should have access to assessment and support.

The UK has one of the highest rates of self-harm in Europe, at 400 per 100,000 population. It is estimated that there are at least 170,000 cases of self-harm which come to hospital attention each year. Many more incidents of self-harming behaviour probably take place but are not included in any statistics because people may choose not to seek medical help.

In the Republic of Ireland, the rate is estimated at 196 per 100,000 population. Over 10,000 cases of parasuicide are seen in Irish hospitals every year.

The group with the highest rates of self-harm are young women aged 15-19 years. In all age groups, females are more likely to self-harm than males.

Young males, however, show the most alarming increases in rates of self-harm.

By far the most common method of self-harm which comes to hospital attention is overdose of drugs, most often paracetamol. Reduction in pack sizes of paracetamol sold over the counter in the UK has resulted in reduced self-harm.

In recognition of the seriousness of self-harm, the associated risk of suicide and the considerable distress it causes to individuals and those around them, national strategies have been developed by English, Scottish and Irish government departments within the last three years.

Definition and meanings

'We all have times when we behave self-destructively. We may not recognise it because we are doing perfectly ordinary activities, such as smoking or overeating. People often overwork, for example, to try and lose themselves and avoid being alone with their thoughts and feelings.'

> **Self-harm encompasses a wide variety of behaviours and acts; different terms such as attempted suicide or parasuicide may also be used to describe it**

'Self-harm', 'attempted suicide', 'parasuicide' and 'deliberate self-harm' (or DSH) are all terms which are often, but not always, used interchangeably. They all describe non-fatal acts of self-harm, which arise for a variety of reasons. However, some authors employ subtle differences between the terms.

The WHO definition of 'parasuicide' is as follows – 'An act with non-fatal outcome, in which an individual deliberately initiates a non-habitual behaviour that, without intervention from others, will cause self-harm... and which is aimed at realising changes which the subject desired via the actual or expected physical consequences.'

'Self-harm', unlike parasuicide, can also include habitual behaviours such as self-cutting or poisoning, which usually do not have suicidal intent, although there is the risk of accidental death.

Other definitions of self-harm preclude the wish to die: 'a deliberate non-fatal act whether physical, drug overdosage or poisoning, done in the knowledge that it was potentially harmful and in the case of overdosage that the amount taken was non-fatal.'

For many people, self-harm is a very personal form of expression, one which does not readily invite comment or indeed others' involvement at any level, excepting accidental damage which requires medical intervention.

Literature on self-harm is limited in two ways. First, the data come largely from studies on people who have come to hospital attention as a result of the self-harm, whereas up to 33% of cases may not lead to medical contact. Second, most research has been conducted on deliberate self-poisoning rather than other forms of self-harm such as self-cutting. There is some overlap between these behaviours, but caution should be taken about generalising.

The term 'self-harm' in the title of this article encompasses all of the behaviours – from those with high suicidal intent, through to those acts which are aimed at coping with overwhelming feelings, and which may be more habitual. Where authors of research have used specific

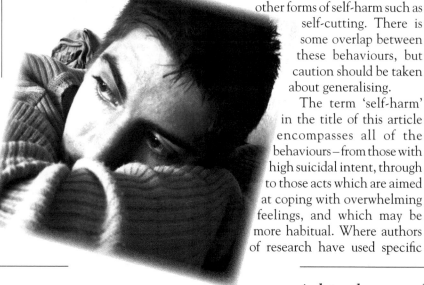

terms, these have been employed within the article. Care must be used when reviewing research data because different authors may employ the same term differently.

Wish to die vs. coping strategy

Self-harm can involve different degrees of risk to life, ranging from a wish to die through to self-harm being used as a coping strategy which allows the person to carry on living. The acts can range from high degree of seriousness resulting in coma, irreversible damage, need for intensive care, through to physical injuries which do not require medical attention.

The act itself is not necessarily a good predictor of the intentions of the self-harmer. One study found that 'seriousness' of self-harm (measured by factors such as: the method used; the degree of damage – e.g. deep coma; extent of lesions or toxicity etc.; degree of reversibility of effects; type of treatment required – e.g. intensive care) – was not related to measure of suicidal intent reported by the person. Depression and impulsivity correlated more highly with the strength of the intent to die by suicide.

Acts of self-harm, particularly habitual self-injury such as self-cutting, are often seen by others as manipulative or attention-seeking. However those who do self-harm have usually lived through very difficult and painful experiences and describe their behaviour as a way of coping with overwhelming feelings and gaining a sense of control.

Australian research on people who habitually self-harm has shown that psychophysiological and psychological tension is reduced as a result of self-harming. However, after a person stops engaging in this behaviour, the tension-reducing feelings associated with the act are open to reinterpretation.

People who self-harm by injurious methods such as cutting, scratching, biting, burning etc., often report that they wish they could stop. The behaviour may start as a method of coping but become a compulsion and problem in its own right.

Personal account of self-harm:

'There is such a rush from doing it, such a relaxation and relief, that you do not actually feel anything. It is the one thing that only I can decide – whether to pick up a knife or hit the wall, how much pain I am going to inflict.'

Risk of suicide

The suicide risk among self-harm patients who come to hospital attention is many times higher than in the general population. After one year, around 15% of people who self-harm come back to hospital having repeated the self-harm. The strong connection between self-harm and later suicide lies somewhere between 0.5% and 2% after one year and above 5% after nine years.

Self-harm can involve different degrees of risk to life, ranging from a wish to die through to self-harm being used as a coping strategy which allows the person to carry on living

---

Scandinavian research found that in all age groups, suicide rates amongst those who had self-harmed were 15 to 300 times greater than the general population.

Several studies have shown that approximately one out of every 100 people who are seen at hospital for self-harm will die by suicide within a year of the self-harm. This is a suicide risk approximately 100 times that of the general population.

Following one act of self-harm which comes to hospital attention, the highest risk of suicide is during the first three years, especially in the first six months following the self-harm. Factors associated with suicide risk include being male; being older (for females); psychiatric disorder (especially schizophrenia); long-term use of sleep-inducing drugs; poor physical health and repeated self-harm.

Repeated self-harm is an important phenomenon and recent research shows the following risks for those who have been seen at hospital for self-harm:
⇨ 39% of people attending A&E for self-inflicted harm repeated the behaviour.
⇨ Those who repeated were at greater risk of suicide than those who self-harmed once.
⇨ Although overall suicide risks are higher for males, females who repeatedly self-harm are at relatively higher risk of dying by suicide compared to those who self-harm once only.
⇨ In males repetition of self-harm is not such a high risk factor.
⇨ Relative risk decreases with increasing age up to 54 years.

⇨ Previous self-harm is a potent risk factor for subsequent suicide, even if it occurred many years ago.

A Scottish study found that:

⇨ 31.6% of people were readmitted with further episodes of deliberate self-harm.

⇨ 2.6% died by suicide, all of these deaths occurred more than five years after the initial episode.

⇨ The risk of suicide, compared with the general population, is higher in all age groups.

⇨ Accidental deaths in men and homicide deaths in men and women were also elevated.

⇨ Alcohol misuse was a contributory factor.

Prevalence and trends

In the UK, 170,000 people per year attend hospital for self-poisoning alone.

Rates of self-harm in the UK are among the highest in Europe at 400 per 100,000 per year. Self-harm rose dramatically from the late 1960s to the early 1970s, then decreased in the early 1980s but rose again by the end of the decade.

Women are more likely than men to self-harm, however, whereas women once showed two or three times the male rate, recent increases in self-harm by men have changed the female to male ratio to 1.6:1.

A national survey was carried out in Great Britain in 2000, which asked a large sample of people to report on their behaviour. This gives us some idea of community rates of self-harm and suicidal intentions.

⇨ 4.4% of respondents said they had ever attempted suicide, and 0.5% had attempted suicide in the past year. The highest rates were among younger people (5% of 16- to 24-year-olds, 6% of 25- to 34-year-olds, compared with 2% of 65- to 74-year-olds).

⇨ A further 2% of respondents had self-harmed without suicidal intent. Factors associated with such self-harm were the number of stressful life events, being young (aged 16 to 24), having psychosis, depression or anxiety and dependence on drugs.

⇨ 15% of survey respondents said they had considered suicide at some point in their life; 4% had considered suicide in the past year; 0.4% had considered suicide in the past week.

In a study of 6,020 school pupils in England commissioned by Samaritans, it was found that 6.9% reported an act of deliberate self-harm in the previous year, which met the criteria of initiating behaviour or ingesting substances with the intention to cause self-harm. Of these acts, only 12.6% had received attention at hospital.

There was a substantial increase in rates of self-harm coming to hospital attention between 1985 and 1995 in the UK, with a 62.1% increase in males and a 42.2% increase in females.

The rise was particularly noticeable in young men aged 15-24 years (a rise of 194%) and women aged 25-34 years.

Rates of repetition increased in both males and females, and self-harm rates correlated with suicide rates.

In the Republic of Ireland, self-harm is referred to as parasuicide. It is estimated that over 10,500 parasuicide acts, carried out by over 8,400 people, are seen in hospitals in Ireland every year. This is a rate per 100,000 population of 196.

In Ireland, 42.3% of acts of self-harm are by men, and 57.7% by women. As for the UK, the large majority (72.3%) are overdoses, 18.8% are self-cutting and the rest include drowning, hanging, ingestion of poisons.

As for the UK, in Ireland self-harm is highest among younger people. The peak rate is for young women aged 15-19, at 626 per 100,000. The peak rate for men is at the slightly older age of 20-24, at 407 per 100,000.

Methods used

Self-poisoning is far more common as a method of self-harm compared to self-injury. Of admissions to hospital between 1985 and 1997 in the UK,

⇨ 89% of people (87.4% of episodes) were self-poisoning.

⇨ 7.7% of people (8.9% of episodes) were self-injury.

⇨ 3.3% of people (3.7% of episodes) were both self-poisoning and self-injury.

Paracetamol and paracetamol compound remain the drugs most commonly used in self-poisoning. Half of all overdoses involved paracetamol in 1995.

There were substantial increases in self-poisoning with paracetamol and antidepressants between 1985 and 1997 in the UK.

Paracetamol overdoses were more common in people who self-harm for the first time and young people, antidepressants and tranquillisers more common in people who repeat self-harm and older people.

Degree of suicidal intent may influence choice of method of self-poisoning used; self-poisoning with gas and non-ingestible poisons was associated with high suicidal intent.

In a large multicentre European Study, it was found that overdose was by far the most common method of self-harm, used by men 73% of the time and women 84% of the time. Females took overdoses more often than men; men were more likely to use alcohol, cutting, solvents and pesticides, hanging and throwing self in front of moving object. Drowning was used more often by women.

⇨ The above information is an extract from 'Self-harm and Suicide', information published by Samaritans, and is reprinted with permission. To view the full text and references, or for more information, please visit www.samaritans.org

© Samaritans

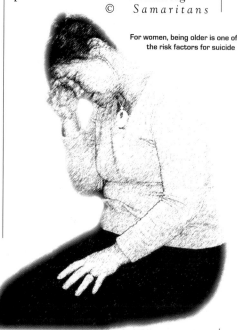

For women, being older is one of the risk factors for suicide

Suicide and attempted suicide

Mental health and growing up

Why do people try to kill themselves?

Nearly everyone has times when they feel sad and lonely. Sometimes, it can feel as if no one really likes us, that we are a failure, that we just upset people and that no one would care if we were dead. We may feel angry but unable to say so, or feel hopeless about the future.

Often, the decision to attempt suicide is made quickly without thinking

---

It is feelings like these that make some young people try to kill themselves. Often, several upsetting things have happened over a short time and one more upset or rejection is the 'last straw'. An argument with parents is a common example; another is breaking up with a friend, or being in trouble. Teenagers who try to kill themselves are often trying to cope independently with very upset feelings, or difficult problems for the first time. They don't know how to solve their problems, or lack the support they need to cope with a big upset. They feel overwhelmed and see no other way out.

Often, the decision to attempt suicide is made quickly without thinking. At the time, many people just want their problems to disappear, and have no idea how to get help. They feel as if the only way out is to kill themselves.

The risk of suicide is higher when a young person:
⇨ is depressed, or when they have a serious mental illness; if they get the help and treatment they need, the risk can be greatly reduced

⇨ is using drugs or alcohol when they are upset
⇨ has tried to kill themselves a number of times or has planned for a while about how to die without being saved
⇨ has a relative or friend who tried to kill themselves.

Is this just attention-seeking?

No. Attempted suicide should always be taken seriously. The young person needs someone to understand what they have been feeling, although they might find it hard to put into words. They need someone to listen, and who is prepared to help.

Who is most at risk?
⇨ There has been an increase in the suicide rate in young men over recent years.
⇨ Many young people who try to kill themselves have mental health and personality problems.
⇨ Suicide attempts in young people nearly always follow a stressful event, usually relationship problems. However, sometimes

the young person will have shown no previous signs of mental health problems.
⇨ Sometimes, the young person has had serious problems (e.g. with the police, their family or school) for a long time. These are the young people who are most at risk of further attempts. Some will already be seeing a counsellor, psychiatrist or social worker. Others have refused normal forms of help, and appear to be trying to run away from their problems.
⇨ Young people who are misusing drugs or alcohol have the highest risk of death by suicide.

How can I help?
⇨ Notice when your child seems upset, withdrawn or irritable.
⇨ Encourage them to talk about their worries. Show them you care by listening, and helping them to find their own solutions to problems.
⇨ Buy blister packs of medicine in small amounts. This helps prevent impulsive suicides after

a row or upset. Getting pills out of a blister pack takes longer than swallowing them straight from a bottle. It may be long enough to make someone stop and think about what they are doing.

⇨ Keep medicines locked away.

⇨ Get help if family problems or arguments keep upsetting you and your child.

For parents, it's hard to cope with a child attempting suicide and it's natural to feel angry, frightened or guilty. It may also be hard to take it seriously or know what to do for the best.

Specialist help

Everyone who has tried to kill themselves, or taken an overdose, needs an urgent assessment by a doctor as soon as possible even if they look OK. The harmful effects can sometimes be delayed. Even small amounts of some medication can be fatal. Poisoning with paracetamol is the most common type of overdose in Britain. Overdosing with paracetamol causes serious liver damage, and each year this leads to many deaths. Even a small number of tablets can be fatal.

All young people who attempt suicide or harm themselves should have a specialist mental health assessment before leaving the hospital. The aim is to discover the causes of the problem. It is usual for parents or carers to be involved in treatment. This makes it easier to understand the background to what has happened, and to work out together whether help is needed.

A lot of young people make another attempt if they do not receive the help they need. Usually, treatment will involve individual or family work for a small number of sessions. A very small number of young people who try to kill themselves really do still want to die. Often, they are suffering from depression or another treatable mental health problem. They may need specialist help over a longer period of time.

⇨ The above information is reprinted with kind permission from the Royal College of Psychiatrists. Visit www.rcpsych.ac.uk for more information.

© *Royal College of Psychiatrists*

Suicide advice

Every moment, someone somewhere is considering taking his or her life. You may know that person. You may even be that person. Susan Quilliam advises

If you are feeling suicidal

Killing yourself can seem a very logical step. You feel depressed. Perhaps your relationship has finished. Maybe you've lost your job. Life just doesn't feel worth living.

The vast majority of people who feel suicidal only do so for a very short time. Then they get the help they need, recover, and begin to enjoy life again

---

No one understands, and it's impossible to tell anyone how you feel. What would they think of you? You hold back, bottle up your feelings and feel even worse.

Reasons to hold back from suicide

1. Hurting inside may make suicide seem justifiable, but it's always helpful to remember that there

are ways to stop hurting. Even if you've tried to get help in the past and failed, there is a way out of the pain – you just haven't found it yet. If you stay alive and keep looking for the support you need, you will find it. There are many people out there who care. The fact is, the vast majority of people who feel suicidal only do so for a very short time. Then they get the help they need, recover, and begin to enjoy life again.

2. Killing yourself may seem justifiable to you, maybe because you feel you're hurting others by being alive, but suicide isn't the answer. If you die, the people you love will feel guilty for the rest of their lives. So if you feel tempted to kill yourself, try pulling back from contact with the people you think you're hurting until you've found resolution to your problem.

It's tough, but it's a more loving way forward. However worried people feel about you, and hurt they are by the way you are now, they'll hurt a lot more if you die.

3. One other reason you may be thinking of killing yourself is to make a point to someone who's hurt you, but that's not rewarding at all. Yes, you'll make your point – but you won't be around to see the impact. If you want to tell them something, do it in a way that allows you to witness the impact you're making. No, don't harm that person. But go and see them. Tell them, to their face, how they've hurt you and what you really think of them. If you've got the courage to kill yourself, use that courage to confront your enemies and defeat them.

What to do now

If you're considering taking your life right now, do one important thing: Wait. Wait for twenty-four hours. Then another twenty-four hours. And try making this stretch to a week.

While you're waiting, tell someone what you're feeling. Talk to a friend. Talk to your family or ring the Samaritans – they are available twenty-four hours a day.

⇨ Samaritans England: 08457 909090;
⇨ Samaritans Ireland: 1850 609090;
⇨ See www.suicide-helplines.org for international numbers.

As you wait and seek support, you'll notice something interesting. The edge will go from the pain. You'll realise that you don't hurt all the time – and that talking through your feelings gives you relief. Sure, the pain may come back – but you can keep it at bay by talking about it, even if for just a few minutes at a time.

Once you start talking about your feelings, and other people start hearing you overcome the pain, you'll get a sense that there's a solution to your problems.

Remember, every problem – even yours – has a solution. You just haven't found that solution yet. But get support and help from other people, and you will find it. The pain will stop. And you can start living again.

How you can help if you know someone who's suicidal?

Possibly you're aware that someone you know is thinking of killing themselves. They've talked about it. They've confided in you. More likely, you're not aware. They're putting out the signals, but you haven't spotted them yet.

So what should you look for? Typically, a person is low, tearful, irritable. Or their eating patterns change, their sleep patterns are disturbed, they're taking less care of themselves, they're exhausted.

Another key could be their situation. There'll usually be some event that's triggered this withdrawal. Loss is a key one – losing a job, losing a partner, bereavement, a major disappointment or illness. If the person has a history of suicide attempts, then you should take it extra seriously.

What you will feel

The first thing you'll feel if you realise someone is suicidal is panic.

It's natural – you want to get it right; you want to save them, you want to help them. You may also get confused. Are you seeing what you think you're seeing?

What should you do or not do? Here are some common beliefs about suicide – and the truth behind them.

1. If a person talks about suicide, they won't do it: Wrong. Talking about problems will make people less likely to kill themselves. But it doesn't mean they definitely won't attempt suicide.
2. If you mention suicide, you will put the idea in a person's head: Wrong again. Mentioning it will allow them to talk about it and so ease the possibility. But you won't do any harm at all by asking.
3. People who think about suicide just want attention: Wrong. They typically want to stop pain – their own or other people's. And typically they only think about suicide because they can't think of another way out. Offer them help and the desire to die will fade.

What you can do

The first thing to do if you suspect someone's suicidal is simply to listen.

Once they begin to talk, they will begin to feel understood. Once they feel understood, they'll regain a slight glimmer of hope that there may be a solution to their problem – and they'll feel less suicidal.

The second thing to do is to get help. Don't try to cope alone. Get the person talking to family, to friends, to their GP who can help with medication, to a counsellor who can help with emotional support. Get them to phone the Samaritans (or phone the Samaritans yourself); they will ring the person and give them support.

The more people you get involved in supporting the suicidal person, the better. You must assume the person's problem to be very big, or they wouldn't feel so desperate. It will probably take a lot of resources to sort it out, but you should strive on.

The first thing to do if you suspect someone's suicidal is simply to listen

---

PS: If you're helping a suicidal person, you should try and get help yourself to avoid becoming stressed. Suicide is a very straining issue. Do phone the Samaritans, if necessary, and allow them to support you.

Remember: Samaritans England: 08457 909090; Samaritans Ireland 1850 609090. Outside Britain, log on to www.suicide-helplines.org for your national numbers.

⇨ The above information is re-printed with kind permission from iVillage UK. Visit www.iVillage.co.uk for more information.

© iVillage UK

The warning signs of suicide

Suicide is rarely a spur-of-the-moment decision. In the days and hours before people kill themselves, there are usually clues and warning signs

The strongest and most disturbing signs are verbal – 'I can't go on,' 'Nothing matters any more' or even 'I'm thinking of ending it all.' Such remarks should always be taken seriously.

> **The strongest and most disturbing signs are verbal – 'I can't go on,' 'Nothing matters any more' or even 'I'm thinking of ending it all.' Such remarks should always be taken seriously**

Other common warning signs include:
⇨ Becoming depressed or withdrawn
⇨ Behaving recklessly
⇨ Getting affairs in order and giving away valued possessions
⇨ Showing a marked change in behaviour, attitudes or appearance
⇨ Abusing drugs or alcohol
⇨ Suffering a major loss or life change.

The following list gives more examples, all of which can be signs that somebody is contemplating suicide. Of course, in most cases these situations do not lead to suicide. But, generally, the more signs a person displays, the higher the risk of suicide.

Situations
⇨ Family history of suicide or violence
⇨ Sexual or physical abuse
⇨ Death of a close friend or family member
⇨ Divorce or separation, ending a relationship
⇨ Failing academic performance, impending exams, exam results

⇨ Job loss, problems at work
⇨ Impending legal action
⇨ Recent imprisonment or up-coming release.

Behaviours
⇨ Crying
⇨ Fighting
⇨ Breaking the law
⇨ Impulsiveness
⇨ Self-mutilation
⇨ Writing about death and suicide
⇨ Previous suicidal behaviour
⇨ Extremes of behaviour
⇨ Changes in behaviour

Physical changes
⇨ Lack of energy
⇨ Disturbed sleep patterns – sleeping too much or too little
⇨ Loss of appetite

⇨ Sudden weight gain or loss
⇨ Increase in minor illnesses
⇨ Change of sexual interest
⇨ Sudden change in appearance
⇨ Lack of interest in appearance.

Thoughts and emotions
⇨ Thoughts of suicide
⇨ Loneliness – lack of support from family and friends
⇨ Rejection, feeling marginalised
⇨ Deep sadness or guilt
⇨ Unable to see beyond a narrow focus
⇨ Daydreaming
⇨ Anxiety and stress
⇨ Helplessness
⇨ Loss of self-worth.

If you are worried about someone you know, make sure you read the how to help pages on the Befrienders Worldwide website.

⇨ The above information is reprinted with kind permission from Befrienders Worldwide. Visit www.befrienders.org for more information.

© *Samaritans UK and ROI*

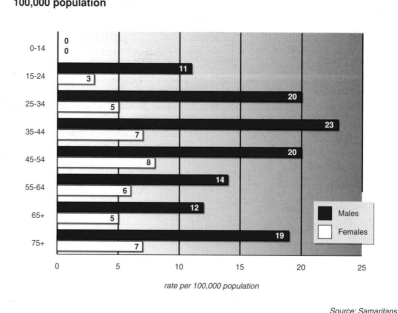

Suicide rate by age group

Suicide and undetermined deaths by age group and gender, UK, 2004. Rate per 100,000 population

Age group	Males	Females
0-14	0	0
15-24	11	3
25-34	20	5
35-44	23	7
45-54	20	8
55-64	14	6
65+	12	5
75+	19	7

rate per 100,000 population

Source: Samaritans.

Lowest suicide rate since records began

New report also shows suicide rate for young men is continuing to fall steadily

The national suicide rate is at its lowest level since records began, according to the third annual report of the National Suicide Prevention Strategy published today. The report also shows a sustained drop in the number of young men committing suicide – which is the first sustained downward trend for 25 years – and a drop in the number of suicides among prisoners and mental health in-patients.

The report shows the most recent suicide rate (for the three years 2002/3/4) was 8.56 deaths per 100,000 population – a reduction of 6.6% from the 1995/6/7 baseline. The target is to reduce the suicide rate by at least a fifth by the year 2010 (from the baseline rate of 9.2 deaths per 100,000 population in 1995/6/7 to 7.3 deaths per 100,000 population in 2009/10/11).

The report, which was jointly produced by the Department of Health and the National Institute for Mental Health in England (NIMHE), outlined specific areas where progress is being made:

⇨ the ongoing development of three mental health promotion pilots aimed at young men in Camden, Manchester and Bedfordshire

⇨ the commissioning of research into the risk of suicide and self harm amongst lesbian, gay and bisexual people and a separate research project looking at suicide risk amongst different ethnic minority groups

⇨ the phased withdrawal of the commonly prescribed painkiller co-proxamol

⇨ the three-centre study of deliberate self-harm to help provide accurate data, trends and patterns to enable effective interventions to be developed.

The target is to reduce the suicide rate by at least a fifth by the year 2010

Health minister Rosie Winterton said:

'Suicide is a major cause of preventable death in England and elsewhere. At a personal level, suicide is a terrible and needless tragedy, and each death is a loss to society.

'The sustained decline in the suicide rate for young men is welcome. This shows that our suicide prevention strategy is having a real impact on the vulnerable people who most need help.'

National director for mental health Professor Louis Appleby said:

'The fall in in-patient suicides is particularly encouraging news. In-patient safety has been a real focus for the NHS, including the introduction of specific measures such as better risk management, appropriate care and treatment for people who self-harm and removal of ligature points from which hangings could occur.

'Whilst these figures are positive, we must work hard to ensure that this downward trend continues. Changes in the suicide rate reflect the mental health of the community and every action we take to improve mental health services will help reduce these numbers further.

Priorities for the next year include:

⇨ developing and publishing guidance on actions to be taken at hotspots for suicide

⇨ improving the way suicide and suicidal behaviour is portrayed in the media

⇨ promoting the successful intervention measures arising out of the evaluation of the mental health promotion pilots aimed at young men

⇨ publishing an information and support pack for people bereaved by sudden traumatic death, including suicide

⇨ encourage mental health services to provide early follow-up to high risk patients who are discharged from hospital

⇨ implementing the NICE guidance on Depression and Self-harm

⇨ continuing to implement Delivering Race Equality in Mental Health Care, the five-year action plan for achieving equality and tackling discrimination in mental health services in England

⇨ taking forward the mental health promotion aspects of the White Paper *Choosing Health*.

13 April 2006

⇨ The above information is reprinted with kind permission from the Department of Health. Visit www.dh.gov.uk for more information.

One life lost every 40 seconds

World Suicide Prevention Day 10th September 2006, promoting new hope

Globally, every three seconds someone attempts to take his or her own life and almost one million deaths a year are by suicide. This is higher than the total number of deaths each year from homicide and road accidents combined. Since the year 2000 there have been more than five million suicide deaths worldwide. Suicide is an important public health problem and is a leading cause of death amongst teenagers and young adults.

The International Association for Suicide Prevention (IASP) in collaboration with the World Health Organization (WHO) is using Sunday 10th September to draw attention to suicide as a leading cause of premature and preventable death. The theme for this year's World Suicide Prevention Day is 'with understanding, new hope' and the focus is on translating current scientific knowledge and research about suicidal behaviour into practical programmes and activities that can reduce suicidal behaviour.

Samaritans Chief Executive, David King, said: 'We support World Suicide Prevention Day through our vision for a society where fewer people die by suicide. It is vital that there is greater understanding of suicide awareness to reduce stigma and save lives.'

In January this year, lawyer Katherine Ward took her own life by jumping from a hotel window ledge in Kensington. Her close friend Marina Palomba said: 'None of her friends or I had any inkling that she was depressed or that anything was remotely wrong. She was a brilliant lawyer with an excellent job, a beautiful home in South Kensington and lots of travel to wonderful places. She had many good friends but she had divorced many years ago and

SAMARITANS

she did not have children. She was still so young and attractive, just over 50, though she looked no more than 40.'

Only two months before her death Katherine had spent a happy week in Prague with other friends and colleagues. Marina said: 'Of all the people I know, she was the most self-possessed, confident and able.

'We were all shocked and perplexed by what happened and it was such an awful and truly tragic waste of life, for no reason at all. It is awful not to have a reason or excuse for what happened. It would be nice to help explain her death. Some obvious reason, some excuse.

Since the year 2000 there have been more than five million suicide deaths worldwide

---

'It is beyond my comprehension to even try to imagine how depressed and without hope she must have been to have killed herself in such an awful manner. The irony was because she was such a good actress none of us suspected how she was feeling and so perhaps did not help as much as we could have done had we known.

'Kath has left a huge void in the life of all her friends. I will never forget her or the awful day after New Year that she died so unnecessarily.'

Samaritans branches are promoting World Suicide Prevention Day by holding events and initiatives around September 10th. Some

have chosen to hold their own local media conferences linked with other agencies involved in suicide reduction while others are holding volunteer recruitment days, hosting workshops, wearing suicide prevention awareness pins and holding vigils.

Samaritans also coordinates a network of over 400 affiliated Befrienders Worldwide member centres in 40 countries staffed by almost 30,000 volunteers. These volunteers work to give emotional help and reduce suicide. Their work stretches from Zimbabwe to Japan, from Lithuania to Brazil.

In Sri Lanka volunteers are organising a workshop for school children to promote the day; in the USA volunteers are selling suicide prevention awareness pins of purple and turquoise ribbon, with information about warning signs, risk factors and resources, and volunteers in Mauritius are holding a forum debate with the Minister of Social Security, sociologists and NGO representatives to promote suicide awareness after a 12-year-old girl took her own life in Mauritius last week. Bangkok held a rally and published a book of short stories by volunteers.

Integral to our international work is the Samaritans-managed Befrienders Worldwide website, which lists helplines around the world and information on suicide in 21 languages, six of these newly added to mark World Suicide Prevention Day. The site – www.befrienders.org – attracts 80,000 visits a month, half of these being to the foreign-language sections. *8 September 2006*

⇨ The above information is reprinted with kind permission from Samaritans. Visit www.samaritans.org for more information.

© *Samaritans*

Gender split in suicide risk factors

Information from Adfero

The factors increasing the risk that a depressed person will commit suicide are different between men and women, researchers have found.

Scientists at Columbia University have highlighted some of the risk factors that can encourage a depressed person to attempt suicide and noted that men and women are vulnerable to different stresses, Reuters reports.

The factors increasing the risk that a depressed person will commit suicide are different between men and women, researchers have found

---

Writing in the *American Journal of Psychiatry*, they note that men are more likely to take their own lives, while women are at a greater risk of suicidal behaviour.

The research examined 184 women and 130 men who had received treatment for major depression, evaluating them at three months, one year and two years after discharge.

After two years, four of the group had taken their own life and 48 attempted suicide, representing 16.6 per cent of the group.

Women were almost twice as likely to attempt suicide and their risk of completing a suicide attempt was increased six-fold if they had a history of attempts.

They were also at an increased risk of suicide if they displayed suicidal thoughts, hostility, subjective depressive symptoms, borderline personality disorder, smoked and had fewer perceived reasons for living.

After further study, it was found that previous attempts, suicidal thoughts and smoking were all independently associated with an increased suicide risk in women.

For men, the risk of suicide was increased by a family history, past drug misuse, smoking, borderline personality disorder and early parental separation.

Following more research, family history and smoking emerged as robust indicators.

Separate research reported in the *Journal of Clinical Psychiatry* also claims that smoking is independently associated with suicide among people with bipolar disorder.
19 January 2007

⇨ The above information is reprinted with kind permission from Adfero. Please visit their website at www.adfero.co.uk for more information.

© Adfero

One in seven 'contemplates suicide'

One in seven Britons has contemplated suicide, according to research published today.

Men are more likely than women to feel suicidal.

And 18- to 30-year-olds are more likely to consider suicide than any other age group.

The YouGov survey of nearly 2,500 people was carried out by ITV1's *This Morning* to launch a week-long mental health special.

While one in seven (14%) said they had seriously considered killing themselves, one in five (22%) had considered self-harm.

Of those who had thought of taking their own life, 41% were in the 18-30 age group.

One in seven (13%) said they are currently suffering from depression.

Work stress is the most common cause of depression, cited by 46% of men and 28% of women.

Other causes include marriage or relationship breakdown (26%), problems with their children (9%) or addiction to alcohol or drugs (4%).

A further 14% said depression ran in the family.

One in four (24%) said they had been diagnosed by a doctor but received no treatment.

The most successful treatment is a course of anti-depressants, with 27% saying it had helped them overcome the condition.

Another 14% said counselling and cognitive behavioural therapy had alleviated their depression, while 3% cited complementary medicine.

6% of those surveyed said no treatment had been successful.

A *This Morning* spokeswoman said: 'The survey shows that depression is widespread.

'Psychologists have branded January 22 the most depressing day of the year and we thought this was a good time to explore what depression is and what treatments are available.'
22 January 2007

© Press Association

Scotland has the highest suicide rates in Britain

The Office for National Statistics published figures detailing the number of men and women who took their own life.

It also showed the highest suicide rates for both men and women were in Scotland.

Figures for 2002-2004 showed that north of the border the suicide rate was 30 men per 100,000 and 10 women for every 100,000.

That is almost double the rates for England – which were 16.7 per 100,000 for men and 5.4 per 100,000 for females.

North of the border the suicide rate was 30 men per 100,000 and 10 women for every 100,000. That is almost double the rates for England

---

It comes despite the Scottish Executive launching a national suicide prevention strategy in 2002 called Choose Life.

The figures also found that 17 of the 20 areas with the highest male suicide rates between 1998 and 2004 were in Scotland.

The Shetland Isles had the highest rate for male suicides, with 47.5 per 100,000 of the population – more than double the overall UK rate of 19.5 per 100,000.

In addition 12 of the 20 areas with the highest rates for females were also north of the border.

Glasgow had the highest rate for female suicides, with 15.8 per 100,000 – more than two and a half times the overall UK rate of six per 100,000.

Tories said the figures showed the need to look at the reasons behind suicide.

'In recent years more young men are dying at their own hand than are killed in road traffic accidents,' Dave Petrie, the party's communities spokesman, said.

'Ministers must further encourage a culture change to overcome the macho attitude towards illness, addressing the embarrassment and stigma that young men feel about seeking help, particularly with mental health problems. Men must be encouraged to talk about problems and go to their GPs.'

He also said the NHS should focus on preventative care so that people were encouraged to tackle problems early.

A spokeswoman for the Scottish Executive said: 'We have known for some time that Scotland has the highest rates of suicide in the whole of the UK.

'We are committed to tackling this and this is why we set up Choose Life, our national suicide prevention strategy, in 2002.'

She added there were now Choose Life coordinators in all 32 council areas and each had implemented a suicide prevention plan.

Choose Life has been running campaigns targeted at men as almost 75% of suicides are males.

In addition a free and confidential advice line, called Breathing Space, was set up in 2002, complementing Choose Life's suicide prevention work.

The spokeswoman added: 'Encouragingly, most recent figures have shown an 8.6% decrease in suicides from last year and the number of suicides in 2005 was the lowest reported since 1991.

'Also, figures since 2000 suggest there may be an emerging downward trend in suicides in Scotland, but it is too early to tell if we are starting to see a significant trend.'

She concluded: 'Every suicide is a tragedy and suicide prevention should be everyone's business if we are to reduce rates further.'

Isabella Goldie, Scottish head of the Mental Health Foundation, said the figures were concerning.

'Whilst we can partly put this down to socio-economic issues such as poverty, homelessness, drugs and alcohol, action is evidently needed,' she said.

'The Scottish Executive's Choose Life strategy has done some good work but needs to do more to address what is a complex problem.

'Work needs to be done with schools, prisons, employers, equality groups and emergency services to prevent people taking their own lives.'

Ms Goldie stressed the need for early intervention and for services to work together at community level to tackle the stigma that prevents many people from seeking help.

30 August 2006

© *Press Association*

THE FIRST STEP

Suicides

Rate in UK men continues to fall

The suicide rate in men aged 15 and over showed a downward trend during the 1990s, until a sharp increase in 1998. Since this peak, the rate has fallen again. In 2005, the rate was the lowest throughout the period 1991 to 2005, at 17.5 suicides per 100,000 population. Rates in women were lower than those seen in men throughout 1991 to 2005, and were relatively stable across this period at around six suicides per 100,000 population.

In 2005, there were 5,671 suicides in adults aged 15 and over in the UK, which represented one per cent of all adult deaths. Almost three-quarters of these suicides were among men

In 2005, there were 5,671 suicides in adults aged 15 and over in the UK, which represented one per cent of all adult deaths. Almost three-quarters of these suicides were among men, and this division between the sexes was broadly similar throughout the period 1991 to 2005.

In the early 1990s the highest UK suicide rates were in men aged 75 and over, however, this age group had the biggest percentage decrease in rates between 1991 and 2005. Since 1997 the highest rates have been in the 15-44 age group.

This pattern was not the same in women, as those aged 15-44 had the lowest suicide rates throughout 1991 to 2005. Rates for women aged 75 and over had the largest percentage decrease during this period, and in 2005 their suicide rate was only slightly higher than for those aged

15-44. For women, the highest suicide rate in 2005 was in those aged 45-74.

Sources

Office for National Statistics, General Register Office for Scotland, Northern Ireland Statistics and Research Agency.

Notes

Rates are based on deaths registered each year and are directly age-standardised using the European Standard Population.

Suicide has been defined as deaths given an underlying cause of intentional self-harm or injury/ poisoning of undetermined intent. In England and Wales, it has been customary to assume that most injuries and poisonings of undetermined intent are cases where the harm was self-inflicted, but there was insufficient evidence to prove that the deceased deliberately intended to kill themselves. For comparability, this definition has been used across all countries of the UK.

Suicide trends and geographical variations in the United Kingdom from 1991 to 2004 were published in an article in *Health Statistics Quarterly* 31 in August 2006. Results from this article are available via the related link.

Published on 22 February 2007

⇨ The above information is re-printed with kind permission from the Office for National Statistics. Visit www.statistics.gov.uk for more information.

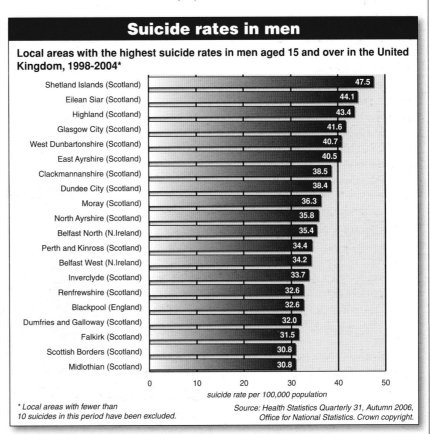

Suicide rates in men

Local areas with the highest suicide rates in men aged 15 and over in the United Kingdom, 1998-2004*

Local area	suicide rate per 100,000 population
Shetland Islands (Scotland)	47.5
Eilean Siar (Scotland)	44.1
Highland (Scotland)	43.4
Glasgow City (Scotland)	41.6
West Dunbartonshire (Scotland)	40.7
East Ayrshire (Scotland)	40.5
Clackmannanshire (Scotland)	38.5
Dundee City (Scotland)	38.4
Moray (Scotland)	36.3
North Ayrshire (Scotland)	35.8
Belfast North (N.Ireland)	35.4
Perth and Kinross (Scotland)	34.4
Belfast West (N.Ireland)	34.2
Inverclyde (Scotland)	33.7
Renfrewshire (Scotland)	32.6
Blackpool (England)	32.6
Dumfries and Galloway (Scotland)	32.0
Falkirk (Scotland)	31.5
Scottish Borders (Scotland)	30.8
Midlothian (Scotland)	30.8

* Local areas with fewer than 10 suicides in this period have been excluded.

Source: Health Statistics Quarterly 31, Autumn 2006, Office for National Statistics. Crown copyright.

New drive to reduce suicide rate for young men

Information from the Department of Health

A new drive to reduce the suicide rates in young men was launched today by Health Minister Rosie Winterton. Speaking to mark Men's Mental Health week, she published a report outlining the findings of three pilots which have been looking at ways to reduce suicide rates in young men.

Suicide is the most common cause of death in young men – last year almost 1,000 young men took their own lives

---

Suicide is the most common cause of death in young men, and although the last five years have seen a sustained downward trend in the figures, last year almost 1,000 young men took their own lives. The three government-funded projects were set up in 2004 to help identify the barriers that may discourage young men from seeking help and look at ways of reaching out to this particularly vulnerable group. The results of the pilots, published today, will be used to spread best practice and learning across the NHS.

The pilots – based in Camden, Bedfordshire and Manchester – found that:

⇨ Community-based locations such as youth centres and youth-oriented services offered a more successful means of engaging with young men than more formal settings such as GP surgeries;

⇨ Front-line staff, when given appropriate training, are better able to engage with young men;

⇨ Alternative terms to 'mental health' – such as 'dealing with stress' or 'wellbeing' – need to be adopted to encourage young men to engage with future projects and to ensure that mental health issues are discussed in a non-stigmatising way;

⇨ Proactive and community-based outreach programmes should be established as these approaches were perceived by young men as more acceptable, less threatening to their self-esteem and less risky, since staff were perceived as less likely to share information with other agencies, such as the police; and

⇨ Accessible information and advice needs to be available for family members and friends of young men, since they are likely to provide a more immediate and trusted source of support.

Speaking at the 'Mind Your Head' conference organised by the Men's Health Forum, Rosie Winterton said:

'There is no health without mental health and we are committed to getting this message across to young men. Men are almost three times as likely to take their own life as women. We must do everything we can to prevent these deaths as each case is a needless tragedy for the friends and family of the victim, as well for society.

'Although we have recently seen a fall in the suicide rate amongst young men, we need to work hard to ensure that this downward trend continues. We already have a national suicide strategy that is starting to have an impact but we need to redouble our efforts in getting young men to look after their mental wellbeing and seek help when they need it.

'I am pleased to publish the *Reaching Out* report. The lessons learned by these pilots will help services improve the way they engage young men. I would also like to congratulate the Men's Health Forum for the key work they are doing in promoting mental wellbeing.'

14 June 2006

⇨ The above information is reprinted with kind permission from the Department of Health. Visit www.dh.gov.uk for more information.

Suicide and the media

Information from Befrienders Worldwide

Samaritans UK/ROI believes responsible discussion of suicide on the internet and in the media can lead to a better understanding of suicidal behaviour and the value of expression of feelings. 29% of people in the UK know someone who has taken their own life, and enabling someone to talk openly about suicidal thoughts is an important step in breaking down the taboo.

However, glamorising suicide or providing 'how to' type advice about suicide on the internet, as in other forms of media, is potentially very dangerous. Although there is little research as yet to prove that there is a link between people visiting suicide chat rooms and taking their own lives, research carried out into the portrayal of suicide in traditional media, such as television, magazines and newspapers, shows that there is a direct link between the way in which suicide is discussed and vulnerable people's behaviour. A number of recent cases highlighted in the media seem to indicate that there is a link, but research needs to be carried out to establish the extent and exact nature of it.

Anyone in emotional distress, or actively thinking about suicide is vulnerable and often looking for help in any form. Samaritans strongly encourages anyone publishing material about suicide to follow these guidelines:

⇨ Do not show or explain the method of suicide

⇨ Do not emphasise potential positive results of killing oneself

⇨ Do not trivialise suicide or portray it as an easy way out.

Glamorising suicide or providing 'how to' type advice about suicide on the internet, as in other forms of media, is potentially very dangerous

---

The internet is an important medium for discussion about suicide and for providing support. But it can be difficult to know what the motives of people who are visiting suicide chat rooms or websites are and whether they are being honest in their contributions. Vulnerable people could be influenced by people who are in these cyber spaces for another reason than seeking help or supporting others.

The UK Suicide Act of 1961 states that is illegal to aid, abet, counsel or procure the suicide of another and Samaritans strongly encourages anyone publishing material on the internet to do so in a responsible way.

Samaritans UK/ROI offers confidential, emotional support by email on jo@samaritans.org. Launched in 2002, the number of contacts received by Samaritans' email service in 2003 was nearly 100,000, an increase of 38% from 2002. The Samaritans' and Befrienders' websites are a source of information and support for anyone who wants information about the issues of suicide and how to get help. Evidence suggest that there are many benefits to using the internet as a way of providing support for people in distress.

⇨ The anonymity of communicating by email means that people generally feel less frightened of being judged or rejected than in face-to-face circumstances or through speaking on the phone.

⇨ Many people who cannot access help by phone because they are worried about being heard or the phone number appearing on the bill can get in touch using email.

⇨ Online support helps people in distress to imagine the person answering the email in the most beneficial way possible. For example, those who would prefer someone younger to be answering the email can imagine the volunteer in that way, whilst those who would prefer someone older can imagine someone like that.

⇨ It is recognised that writing is, in itself, a useful tool. The process of writing something down enables people to focus fully on their own feelings without worrying about taking up another person's time or saying the wrong thing.

Samaritans UK/ROI currently has a relationship with the ISP Wanadoo, whereby when anyone types a term into its search engine relating to suicide (e.g. suicide, or I want to kill myself), Samaritans UK/ROI is given a prominent advertisement style listing above their other search results. Samaritans UK/ROI has now replicated this relationship with AOL and we also very much hope that other ISPs and search engine organisations, such as Yahoo and MSN, follow suit.

⇨ The above information is re-printed with kind permission from Befrienders Worldwide. Visit www.befrienders.org for more information.

© Samaritans UK and ROI

Photo: Bruno de Souza Leão

Suicide websites

Call to ban suicide websites as second pupil kills herself

By Nigel Bunyan

Calls for a ban on websites that promote suicide were renewed yesterday after it emerged that a 13-year-old girl had visited such a site before hanging herself.

Jenny Sykes was found by her mother when she went into her bedroom to say she was running late for school.

The teenager was the second pupil at Lytham St Annes High School, Lancs, to commit suicide in eight months.

> **Calls for a ban on websites that promote suicide were renewed after it emerged that a 13-year-old girl had visited such a site before hanging herself**

Paul Moran, who was in the same school year, hanged himself in his bedroom after allegedly being subjected to bullying text messages.

Yesterday Lancashire Police indicated that Jenny, regarded by her parents as 'a normal, happy teenager', had visited a suicide chat room.

The revelation has led to new calls for the 1961 Suicide Act to be strengthened. Campaigners believe its effectiveness has been massively reduced by the advent of the internet.

The Act makes it a crime to aid, abet, counsel or procure another either to kill themselves or to try to do so. But lawyers struggle to prove the causal link between what someone is told on the internet and what they then do.

Tony Cox, of the charity Papyrus, which works to prevent suicide among the young, said: 'This latest death seems to be another example of the danger the internet presents to vulnerable young people and shows how much we need to look at regulating these sites much more closely.

'In the days when the present law was drafted the source of information might have been a book, which would probably have taken some time to acquire. Now it is immediate, and it responds to the impulsiveness of youth.

'There seems to be a sub-culture on the internet, with some people almost grooming others to die. Such people may get some sort of power or buzz from that.

'They might build up a false relationship and then either give the other party a method of taking their own life or say something like, "You don't really belong in this world".'

Paul Kelly, a retired teacher and a trustee of Papyrus, believes that his son, Simon, 18, who died five years ago, was swayed towards ending his life by his contact with a suicide chat room.

Although those in the chat room appeared to have no malevolent intent, their 'pro-choice' stance meant they never made the call to Simon's brother that might have saved his life.

The Samaritans support the call for more stringent policing of suicide chat rooms.

A spokesman urged youngsters to phone, e-mail or even text the organisation if they felt they needed help. A spokesman for the Home Office said: 'The Government understands concerns about these websites and the potential influence that they may have over vulnerable young people.

'This is a complex issue and there is no easy or quick fix. Where these websites are hosted in the UK, if they are breaking the law the prosecuting authorities can take action against those producing them and steps can be taken to remove the illegal material but, however distasteful they may be, what they are doing is not necessarily illegal.'

The Home Office was working with other government departments to see what non-legislative action could be taken to deter sites and make them less easily accessible.

14 July 2006

-YOU'RE PUSHING ME...

Internet suicide pacts

Nine bodies found as Japan fails to curb internet suicide pacts

⇨ *Group victims found poisoned in vehicles*
⇨ *Police discoveries follow record year for 'cybercide'*

Nine people have been found dead in two suspected group suicides in Japan this week, despite efforts to stem an alarming rise in death pacts by people meeting over the internet.

Police discovered the bodies of five men and a woman – all in their 20s – in a van in a forest in Chichibu, 50 miles north-west of Tokyo, yesterday.

> **Suicide pacts may be as old as civilisation itself, but the use of the internet as a macabre matchmaker has sent the incidence soaring in recent years**

They had apparently died from carbon monoxide poisoning, the preferred method of internet suicide victims. Three charcoal burners were found smouldering in the vehicle. Last night, officers were trying to identify the six, and believed they had arranged to die together after meeting via an online chatroom for people contemplating suicide.

The bodies of two men and a woman in their 20s and 30s were found in similar circumstances in Aomori prefecture in northern Japan on Wednesday. The three had reportedly hatched plans to die together after meeting in hospital.

A record 91 Japanese died in 34 'cybercides' in 2005, according to police – up from 55

By Justin McCurry in Tokyo

people a year earlier. The annual number has almost tripled since records began in 2003.

Despite the increase, authorities claim to have prevented several group suicides under new regulations that require website operators to pass on the contact details of people believed to be at risk.

Internet suicides have occurred in several countries, including Britain, the Netherlands and South Korea, but the incidence has grown rapidly in Japan, which has one of the world's highest overall suicide rates. In 2004, more than 32,000 Japanese killed themselves.

News of the latest cases came as the Japanese defence agency said a record number of troops had killed themselves last year – some of them after tours of duty in Iraq, Japan's biggest military deployment since the second world war.

The agency said that 94 military personnel had committed suicide in the 12 months to March 31 2005 – up from 75 the previous year. At 37 suicides per 100,000

people, the death rate in the military is well above the national average of 24 per 100,000.

Three of the soldiers killed themselves after returning from southern Iraq, where 2,400 Japanese troops have taken part in a humanitarian mission since early 2004. 'It isn't clear whether the suicides were connected to their mission in Iraq,' a defence spokesman told the Kyodo news agency.

The Japanese government has sent psychiatric experts to Iraq to counsel soldiers worried about being targeted in terrorist attacks. Counselling is also available to those who have returned home.

Backstory

Suicide pacts may be as old as civilisation itself, but the use of the internet as a macabre matchmaker has sent the incidence soaring in recent years. Cases have been reported all over the world, including in Britain last September when two strangers killed themselves in a car park after meeting via a suicide chatroom.

Most instances have happened in Japan. Groups usually number between two and four people in their 20s or 30s. Suicide counsellors say chatrooms embolden the suicidal by providing strength in numbers, practical tips and a dangerous 'group think' that can reinforce a sense of hopelessness.

Some websites have been closed down by their internet service providers, but suicide chatrooms are never more than a simple internet search away. One typical submission to a website yesterday asked: 'Anybody there? I need some help. How can I kill myself tonight without any pain?'

⇨ First published in the *Guardian*, 11 March 2006.
© *Justin McCurry 2006*

⇨ A person who self-harms is likely to have gone through very difficult, painful experiences as a child or young adult. At the time, they probably had no one they could confide in, so didn't receive the support and the emotional outlet they needed to deal with it. (page 1)

⇨ Because it can be hard to understand, healthcare professionals, friends and relatives sometimes mistakenly regard people who self-harm with mistrust or fear and see their behaviour as attention-seeking and manipulative. (page 2)

⇨ 82.4% of young people surveyed for the *Truth Hurts* report had contacted a friend concerning their self-harm. (page 3)

⇨ Although some very young children are known to self-harm and some adults too, the available research evidence indicates that average age of onset is 12 years old. (page 4)

⇨ A hidden epidemic of self-harm is affecting teenagers across Britain, with one adolescent in 12 deliberately injuring themselves on a regular basis. (page 5)

⇨ Research shows that over 40 per cent of adults think young people who self-harm are attention-seeking, one in three feel they are manipulative and 15 per cent believe it is the sign of a failed suicide attempt. (page 6)

⇨ One in ten teenage girls self-harm each year and the problem is far more widespread than was previously thought, shows the largest-ever study of self-harm amongst 15- and 16-year-olds in England. (page 7)

⇨ Young people who self-harm usually feel very guilty and ashamed of what they do, and do not want to talk about it. The stigma associated with self-harm is unhelpful, and stops people getting the support and information they need to find better and more helpful ways of coping. (page 9)

⇨ A history of self-harm is one of the risk factors amongst people who go on to complete suicide. (page 11)

⇨ 85.2% of young people surveyed for the *Truth Hurts* report would want one-to-one support or counselling on offer if they were to seek help for their self-harming. (page 13)

⇨ Self-harm affects at least one in 15 young people. (page 17)

⇨ Some evidence suggests that rates of self-harm in the UK are higher than anywhere else in Europe. (page 17)

⇨ There are widespread misunderstandings among professionals and relatives that prevent young people from getting support and seeking help. Many turn to friends their own age rather than ask for assistance from adults who, if they are asked for help, often react inappropriately. (page 23)

⇨ 39% of people attending A&E for self-inflicted harm repeated the behaviour. (page 25)

⇨ In the UK, 170,000 people per year attend hospital for self-poisoning alone. (page 26)

⇨ Everyone who has tried to kill themselves, or taken an overdose, needs an urgent assessment by a doctor as soon as possible even if they look OK. The harmful effects can sometimes be delayed. (page 28)

⇨ The strongest and most disturbing warning signs of suicide are verbal – 'I can't go on,' 'Nothing matters any more' or even 'I'm thinking of ending it all.' Such remarks should always be taken seriously. (page 30)

⇨ The national suicide rate is at its lowest level since records began, according to the third annual report of the National Suicide Prevention Strategy published in April 2006. (page 31)

⇨ The most recent suicide rate (for the three years 2002/3/4) was 8.56 deaths per 100,000 population – a reduction of 6.6% from the 1995/6/7 baseline. The target is to reduce the suicide rate by at least a fifth by the year 2010. (page 31)

⇨ Globally, every three seconds someone attempts to take his or her own life and almost one million deaths a year are by suicide. This is higher than the total number of deaths each year from homicide and road accidents combined. (page 32)

⇨ The factors increasing the risk that a depressed person will commit suicide are different between men and women, researchers have found. (page 33)

⇨ One in seven Britons has contemplated suicide. (page 33)

⇨ The highest suicide rates for both men and women were in Scotland. (page 34)

⇨ The suicide rate in men aged 15 and over showed a downward trend during the 1990s, until a sharp increase in 1998. Since this peak, the rate has fallen again. (page 35)

⇨ Suicide is the most common cause of death in young men – last year almost 1,000 young men took their own lives. (page 36)

GLOSSARY

Alternate harming techniques

Those who wish to stop self-harming may use alternate harming techniques which don't leave a mark instead of hurting themselves, for example holding ice cubes in the crook of the elbow, or drawing on the skin with red pen.

Overdose

Taking medicine or drugs in amounts which can cause serious damage to health, or death. Overdosing on drugs (most often paracetamol) is the most common method of self-harm which comes to hospital attention.

Risk factors

Characteristics, conditions or behaviours which increase the likelihood of something happening. Risk factors for self-harm include being young (16-24), female, drug or alcohol-dependent, facing a number of major life problems and having previously suffered trauma or abuse. Risk factors for suicide include being male, having self-harmed in the past, being older (if female), having mental health problems or a personality disorder and being faced with stressful events or life problems.

Self-destructive behaviours

Self-harm is one form of self-destructive behaviour; although self-inflicted, it is dangerous and harmful. Other behaviours which are self-destructive include eating disorders, taking dangerous illegal drugs, excessive alcohol intake, smoking, and even overworking or overeating.

Self-harm

Self-harm is a way of expressing very deep distress. It can also be referred to as self-injury, self-abuse, parasuicide or self-mutilation. People may injure or poison themselves by scratching, cutting or burning their skin, by hitting themselves against objects, taking a drug overdose, or swallowing or putting other things inside themselves. Although those who self-harm are at higher risk of suicide, deliberate self-harm is not usually an attempt to end one's own life. Many who self-harm describe it as a coping mechanism: a way of staying alive. Self-harm is more prevalent among young women than men, with recent research suggesting one in ten teenage girls self-harm each year.

Suicide

Suicide is a form of self-harm; it is the deliberate ending of one's own life. When an attempt to kill oneself is unsuccessful, this is referred to as attempted suicide. The rate of suicide in the UK is falling, with the suicide rate currently standing at 8.56 deaths per 100,000 population. However, recent research suggests that as many as one in seven people has contemplated committing suicide. Men are far more likely to commit suicide than women.

Additional Resources

Other Issues titles

If you are interested in researching further some of the issues raised in *Self-Harm*, you may like to read the following titles in the **Issues** series:

⇨ Vol. 132 *Child Abuse* (ISBN 978 1 86168 378 6)

⇨ Vol. 127 *Eating Disorders* (ISBN 978 1 86168 366 3)

⇨ Vol. 125 *Understanding Depression* (ISBN 978 1 86168 364 9)

⇨ Vol. 123 *Young People and Health* (ISBN 978 1 86168 362 5)

⇨ Vol. 122 *Bullying* (ISBN 978 1 86168 361 8)

⇨ Vol. 117 *Self-Esteem and Body Image* (ISBN 978 1 86168 350 2)

⇨ Vol. 114 *Drug Abuse* (ISBN 978 1 86168 347 2)

⇨ Vol. 108 *Domestic Violence* (ISBN 978 1 86168 328 1)

⇨ Vol. 100 *Stress and Anxiety* (ISBN 978 1 86168 314 4)

⇨ Vol. 93 *Binge Drinking* (ISBN 978 1 86168 301 4)

⇨ Vol. 84 *Mental Wellbeing* (ISBN 978 1 86168 279 6)

For more information about these titles, visit our website at www.independence.co.uk/publicationslist

Useful organisations

You may find the websites of the following organisations useful for further research:

⇨ Befrienders Worldwide: www.befrienders.org

⇨ Department of Health: www.dh.gov.uk

⇨ Mental Health Foundation: www.mentalhealth.org.uk

⇨ Mind: www.mind.org.uk

⇨ National Inquiry into Self-harm among Young People: www.selfharmuk.org

⇨ Royal College of Nursing: www.rcn.org.uk

⇨ Royal College of Psychiatrists: www.rcpsych.ac.uk

⇨ Samaritans: www.samaritans.org

ACKNOWLEDGEMENTS

The publisher is grateful for permission to reproduce the following material.

While every care has been taken to trace and acknowledge copyright, the publisher tenders its apology for any accidental infringement or where copyright has proved untraceable. The publisher would be pleased to come to a suitable arrangement in any such case with the rightful owner.

Chapter One: Self-Injury

Understanding self-harm, © Mind, *Self-harm and young people*, © Mental Health Foundation, *Teenagers' epidemic of self-harm*, © Guardian Newspapers Ltd, *Girls and self-harm*, © University of Bath, *Myths and stereotypes*, © Camelot Foundation and the Mental Health Foundation, *Hurting themselves*, © Channel 4, *Talking about self-harm*, © Camelot Foundation and the Mental Health Foundation, *My self-harm story*, © TheSite.org, *Truth hurts*, © Camelot Foundation and the Mental Health Foundation, *Self-harm and Scotland's older people*, © Scotsman, *Stop self-harming*, © TheSite.org, *Minimising self-harm damage*, © TheSite.org, *Health professionals 'misunderstand self-harm'*, © Royal College of Nursing, *Self-harm and suicide*, © Samaritans.

Chapter Two: Suicide

Suicide and attempted suicide, © Royal College of Psychiatrists, *Suicide advice*, © iVillage UK, *The warning signs of suicide*, © Samaritans UK and ROI, *Lowest suicide rate since records began*, © Crown copyright is reproduced with the permission of Her Majesty's Stationery Office, *One life lost every 40 seconds*, © Samaritans, *Gender split in suicide risk factors*, © Adfero, *One in seven 'contemplates suicide'*, © Press Association, *Scotland has the highest suicide rates in Britain*, © Scotsman, *Suicides*, © Crown copyright is reproduced with the permission of Her Majesty's Stationery Office, *New drive to reduce suicide rate for young men*, © Crown copyright is reproduced with the permission of Her Majesty's Stationery Office, *Suicide and the media*, © Samaritans UK and ROI, *Suicide websites*, © Telegraph Group Ltd, *Internet suicide pacts*, © Justin McCurry.

Illustrations

Pages 1, 14, 21, 29, 38: Simon Kneebone; pages 6, 16, 22, 34: Angelo Madrid; pages 9, 19, 27, 36: Don Hatcher; pages 17, 25: Bev Aisbett.

Photographs

Page 2: Ruben Joye; page 12: Steve Woods; page 23: Meliha Gojak; page 31: Alexander Rist; page 37: Bruno de Souza Leão.

And with thanks to the team: Mary Chapman, Sandra Dennis and Jan Haskell.

Lisa Firth
Cambridge
April, 2007